HORRIBLE GEOGRAPHY

NEW EDITION

STORMY Weather

D1649584

'HORRIBLY GOOD'
MICHAEL PALIN

ANITA GANERI
Illustrated by MIKE PHILLIPS

SCHOLASTIC

Scholastic Children's Books,
Euston House, 24 Eversholt Street,
London NW1 1DB, UK

A division of Scholastic Ltd
London ~ New York ~ Toronto ~ Sydney ~ Auckland
Mexico City ~ New Delhi ~ Hong Kong

First published in the UK by Scholastic Ltd, 1999
This abridged edition published by Scholastic Ltd, 2015

Text © Anita Ganeri, 1999, 2008, 2015
Illustrations © Mike Phillips, 1999, 2008, 2015

Roy Hall's story adapted from an actual account written by Roy Hall.

ISBN 978 1407 16396 3

Printed and bound by CPI Group (UK) Ltd, Croydon, CR0 4YY

2 4 6 8 10 9 7 5 3 1

The right of Anita Ganeri and Mike Phillips to be identified as the author and illustrator of this work respectively has been asserted by them in accordance with the Copyright, Designs and Patents Act, 1988.

CONTENTS

Anita Ganeri has climbed an erupting volcano, swum through shark-infested oceans and sailed round the world solo. IN HER DREAMS!

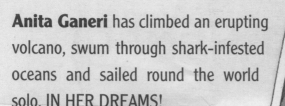

But she was born in far-away India, though she didn't realize it at the time. At school, her only interest in geography was staring out of the classroom window and working out how to escape. Since then, Horrible Geography has grown on her a bit like a mould, and she's even learned to read a map without having to turn it upside down.

Mike Phillips was born... Yippee!! No, I mean he was born in London where he grew up and up and eventually got so big he had to leave. Which is when he discovered his love of travelling, and he set off immediately to tour the world. Nearly thirty years later he has reached North Devon, where he now illustrates the entire world from a sitting position.

4

INTRODUCTION

Geography. It's a big subject, isn't it? In fact, you could say it's gigantic. It means studying the whole wide world – which is almost as big as you can get. Sadly, some teachers have a habit of making geography more boring than a pneumatic drill. They can't help it, that's just how they are. Take a sneaky listen at the staffroom door, and hear how they talk to each other when they're not boring you rigid...

What on earth are they talking about? Well, roughly translated, it's not quite as boring as it sounds. Normal people would say it like this:

Yup, they're talking about the weather — stormy weather to be precise, one of the most horribly interesting bits of geography ever. To find out if there's a storm near you (without even having to get up and turn off the telly), try this simple experiment. Smile sweetly at your mum or dad and ask if they can help you with your geography homework. (They'll be so surprised you've asked, they're bound to agree.) Send them outside for a few minutes, then call them in again. Have a good look at them. Are they...

If the answer is yes to all three questions, stormy weather may be round the corner.

And that's what this book is all about, only it'll say it in language you can understand. Wild enough to lift a train off its tracks, wet enough to drown a town, and windy enough to strip the bark from trees; from terrible tragedies to survival against all odds, stormy weather gets everyone talking. In *Stormy Weather*, you can…

• find out how it feels to be struck by lightning.

- learn how to track a killer tornado.

- fly into the "eye" of a hurricane.

- forecast the weather like a real meteorologist.*

* METEOROLOGIST IS A POSH NAME FOR A GEOGRAPHER WHO STUDIES THE WEATHER, LIKE ME, MONA

- discover that geography isn't so boring after all. In fact, it's horribly exciting. As you're about to find out...

KILLER STORM

Imagine living in the path of a tropical storm. About 500 million people do. Their lives are regularly turned upside down by some of the stormiest weather on the planet. People in some of the world's poorest countries know how it feels to lose everything – their homes, belongings, families. In Central America they tried to piece their lives back together again after they were torn apart in 1998 by Hurricane Mitch. Here's how one survivor of that terrible tragedy might have told her remarkable story…

Honduras, Central America, October-November 1998

My name is Laura Isabel Arriola de Guity. I'm a schoolteacher. At least, I used to be. There aren't any schools round here anymore. I used to live with my husband and three children in a little house in the village of Barra de Aguan, near the mouth of the Aguan river.

But I don't live there anymore.

Thursday, 29 October

What happened was so terrible, it's difficult for me to talk about it. But I'll try. When the great storm came, the water rose like I've never seen before, and the sea came rushing in great waves towards the village.

Many homes were washed away.

Soon the water reached my house too, even though it was half an hour's walk from the sea. My family and I climbed on to our neighbour's roof. We thought we'd be safe there until the water went down.

But we weren't.

The water came and swept us away. We managed to cling to a boat but it was so windy and the waves were so high that we were pulled apart and separated. I never saw my husband and two of my children again.

I myself was thrown into the sea. I was still holding tightly on to my little son but the sea swept him from my arms and took him away from me. I can't talk much about it – it will make me cry. I tried to float so I could see over the water. Then I swam and swam, trying to save him, trying to get somewhere dry. Then I realized I was already in the sea. I was pulled underwater and thought I was going to drown. At that moment, I wanted to die and be with my son. Then a wave pushed me up and swept me further and further out to sea.

I managed to grab some tree roots, branches and a wooden board and tied them together to make a raft. I clung on as best I could. There was rubbish lying all around me: branches and smashed up pieces of houses. I saw many dead animals and the body of a child. But it wasn't one of my children. All the time the sea was carrying me out, further and further, and all the time my heart was breaking in two. It was like a nightmare - the sea was black and cold and I was frightened.

I managed to find some pineapples and oranges to eat and drank some milk from a coconut, but days and days went by and nobody came. All I could see was the sea and the sky. At night I looked at the moon. There wasn't any land anywhere. The sea was very rough and kept knocking me off the raft. And the waves kept pouring over me and I thought I would drown.

I was all alone without anybody. Sometimes I talked to my children and sang them songs to help them sleep. That made me feel closer to them. Sometimes I screamed and shouted with all my might. Every day I cried and cried. But I was all alone and no one heard me.

Wednesday, 4 November – Six days later

One day a little duck swam near my raft and I started to talk to it.

"Little duck, send a message that I'm alive." I told it. "Take me to my people. Take me to the shore." Then I started crying and I said "Why don't you take me with you so that I can fly off with you?" And I prayed to God to bring me help. God must have heard me. Or my dear little duck? I don't know. All I know is that not long afterwards, my prayers were answered. I had fallen asleep and had been dreaming about my children.

Oh, how I wish I could see them and hold them in my arms again. Then I looked up and saw a plane flying above me. It flew away, then a helicopter came and a man came down and pulled me up. I told him, "Thank God you have saved me. Thank God."

I don't know what I will do now. I have nothing. I have nowhere to go. In the storm, I lost it all.

15

Later...

Laura Isabel was rescued by a British Navy ship, HMS *Sheffield*. It had actually been searching for a yacht reported missing in the storm along with its crew of 30, when the coastguard contacted it to say a person had been spotted in the water. The ship's crew couldn't believe that Laura Isabel had survived. She had been swept about 80 kilometres out into the Caribbean Sea and was shivering, cold and very shocked, but amazingly, she wasn't badly injured. She had to fight back the tears as she told her story. Her incredible bravery had pulled her through. One officer said, "To survive in those conditions is absolutely remarkable. I've been in the Navy for 20 years and I've never seen anything like it. Laura Isabel has strength with no equal."

Five stormforce facts about Hurricane Mitch

1 Hurricane Mitch was born in the Caribbean Sea on 22 October 1998. A week later it swept through Central America, hitting Nicaragua, Honduras, El Salvador and Guatemala and leaving a tragic trail of destruction before heading off into the Atlantic on 6 November.

2 Mitch was the worst storm to hit the region in over 200 years. Its howling winds sounded, one survivor said:

LIKE A THOUSAND EXPRESS TRAINS ROARING THROUGH A TUNNEL

3 Thousands of people were killed. Millions of people were left homeless. Worst hit was Honduras – more than half of the country was flooded, three quarters of its farms were ruined and its capital, Tegucigalpa, was completely cut off – no water, no electricity, nothing. Torrential rain caused fatal flooding and murderous mudslides that buried people alive. Even bridges and roads were washed away – the

Pan-American Highway, one of the busiest roads in Central America, collapsed into the valley below.

4 Next time you tuck into a banana, check where it comes from. Before Hurricane Mitch, it probably came from Central America. Then the region's precious rice, banana and coffee crops were devastated by the storm, its plantations covered with a thick sludge of mud. Thousands of people, who had already lost their homes, lost their jobs too.

5 Mitch was not even a very severe hurricane – in fact, by the time it got to Honduras, it was classed as nothing more than a tropical storm. So why on Earth was it so deadly? The rain was one reason. Another was that for years local farmers had been cutting down trees to clear land for crops and grazing. With no roots to hold the soil together, it was easily washed away by the rain. But you can't really blame the farmers. They need the land to grow their food. It's a very vicious circle.

FARMERS CLEAR LAND TO GROW THEIR CROPS...

SOIL WITHOUT ROOTS SOON WASHES AWAY...

PEOPLE ARE LEFT STARVING...

FARMERS NEED TO GROW MORE FOOD...

Hurricane Mitch lasted for ten traumatic days. But it might take decades to repair the damage it caused. An international aid programme was set up, but aid workers found it slow and difficult even to get supplies to people. Sometimes they could only reach people by helicopter and canoe.

Refugee centres were set up for homeless people to shelter in while they tried to rebuild their lives. But most people were — and are still — desperate to go home.

Sadly, there's no guarantee it won't happen again. But how on Earth do these freaky conditions happen? The answer is that even the very stormiest weather is just a lot of hot air.

AWESOME ATMOSPHERE

People love talking about the weather. They stare wisely at the sky and say things like:

> MMM, LOOKS LIKE RAIN

> THERE'S A STORM BREWING. I CAN FEEL IT IN MY BONES.

But what on Earth are they talking about? What on

Earth is the weather? And why on Earth does it happen? Hold on to your hats ...

... because you're about to find out.

What an atmosphere

Go outside and look up. What can you see? High-flying clouds? Low-flying birds? Sky as far as the eye can see? What you can see is the awesome atmosphere, a gigantic blanket of air wrapped around the Earth. It stretches for about 1,000 kilometres above your head (where it starts to merge with space) and you couldn't live without it.

Why? Well, it might look as though it's hanging around doing nothing, but the awesome atmosphere is incredibly useful. Here are two things you wouldn't have without it.

Essential air

Huh, air, you might say, I could live without that, no problem! But you'd be wrong – dead wrong. To stay alive, we human beings need to breathe in oxygen from the air. And where do we get all this essential air from? The awesome atmosphere, of course!

So without the atmosphere, we'd all be dead!

But what's actually in the air we breathe?

A FAIR-WEATHER RECIPE FOR FRESH AIR

SERVES (EVERYONE)

Ingredients:

- Nitrogen (78 per cent)
- Oxygen (21 per cent) – this is the vital bit, the bit you need to keep your body and brain in perfect working order.
- Argon (0·9 per cent)

Other mixed gases (0·1 per cent) – these include carbon dioxide, water vapour and a pinch each of neon, helium, krypton, hydrogen and ozone. Delicious!

What you do:

1. Mix all the gases together.
2. Take a deep breath. Aaahhh! That's better. (but don't forget to breathe out again!)
3. You can make as much air as you like with this recipe, as long as you stick to the percentages given. But if you want to make a full-scale atmosphere, you'll need a mind-boggling 5·5 thousand million million tonnes of air (you can work out the rest yourself!). That's how much the awesome atmosphere weighs.

STORMY WEATHER WARNING ☠

THIS RECIPE IS FOR AIR CLOSE TO THE GROUND, BUT WATCH OUT, IF YOU'RE TREKKING UP A MOUNTAIN. THE HIGHER UP YOU GO, THE LESS OXYGEN THERE IS AND THE HARDER IT IS TO BREATHE.

World weather

You might say, "Hmph, weather! I could definitely live without that." But you'd be wrong again. The weather happens in the bit of atmosphere closest to the Earth.

METEOROLOGISTS CALL IT THE TROPOSPHERE. HERE HEAT FROM THE SUN CHURNS UP THE AIR, MAKING EVERY TYPE OF STORMY WEATHER FROM GENTLE BREEZES TO HOWLING GALES. THE SUN MAY BE 150 MILLION KM AWAY (BLIMEY!) BUT WITHOUT IT THERE WOULD BE NO WEATHER. IT DOESN'T SHINE EVENLY ALL OVER THE WORLD, THOUGH.

Some places are much, much colder than others (especially f-f-freezing geography classrooms). And this is where the weather comes in handy. Its job is to share the heat and cold out. Otherwise, hot places would just get hotter and hotter, and cold places colder and colder, until nothing could live on Earth — including you.

But the troposphere's only the tip of the, ahem, iceberg. There's plenty more atmosphere to come. It's arranged in layers, like a gigantic, a *really* gigantic, sandwich.

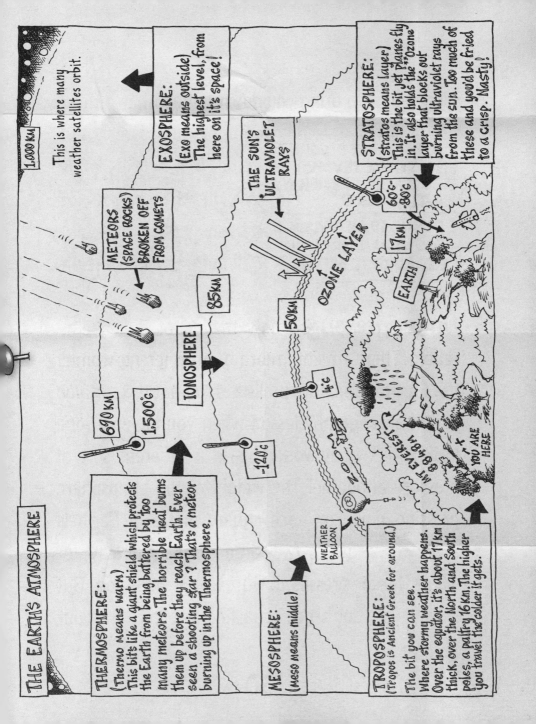

Meanwhile, to bring you down to Earth…

*ULTRAVIOLET SOUNDS QUITE PRETTY, BUT ACTUALLY, THESE RAYS ARE DEADLY!

**OZONE IS AN INVISIBLE GAS—YOU MIGHT HAVE HEARD OF IT BEFORE?

SUN CREAM

Under pressure

With all that air sitting on top of it, it's no wonder the Earth feels under pressure. No, not the sort you feel in a geography lesson when you haven't done last night's homework. This is a different sort of pressure altogether. The weight of the atmosphere pressing down on each square metre of Earth is about the same as two large elephants. Heavy or what! The air presses down on your body too. But luckily, you don't get squashed flat because your breathing balances out the effect.

German geographer, Otto von Guericke (1602–1686) was the first person to show how strong air pressure is.

Otto von Guericke was a bit of a clever clogs. One university degree wasn't enough for him, he had to have three! In law, mathematics and mechanics. He had two careers, too. He was an engineer by day and an astronomer by night. And if that wasn't enough, he even became mayor of a town called Magdeburg in Germany. But swotty Otto is actually best remembered for his famous set of air pressure experiments, called, very excitingly, the Magdeburg experiments. You might want to have a go at these experiments for yourself.

What you will need:
- Two copper cups about 20 centimetres wide
- 16 horses

What you do:
1 Place the cups together to form a hollow ball.
2 Now pump all the air out to make a vacuum.*
3 Divide the horses into two teams of eight.
4 With some rope, tie the ball between the two teams.
5 Stand well clear and shout "Pull!".

(*A vacuum is a completely empty space where there's no air at all, and NOT a machine for sucking up dust. Outer space is a vacuum.)

What do you think happened in the real thing?

a) The cups fell apart and the horses fell over.

b) The cups wouldn't budge.

c) The rope snapped and old clever clogs had to start all over again.

ANSWER

In fact, what happened was **b)**. However hard the horses heaved, they couldn't pull the cups apart. No way. Only when von Guericke pumped some air into the ball did they finally give way. So what on Earth was holding the cups so tightly together? The answer was the air pressing on the outsides. Which shows just how strong air pressure can be.

Pressing discoveries

1 To measure air pressure, meteorologists use a machine called a barometer. There are two main types. Mercury barometers are filled with liquid mercury. Aneroid barometers have a needle and dial instead. They're often used on aeroplanes because they won't break and make a mess on take-off.

2 The first mercury barometer was invented by Italian scientist Evangelista Torricelli (1608–1647), who was professor of maths at Florence University. Here's how he stumbled on the idea:

a) First, he filled a long glass tube with mercury. (He'd already tried seawater and honey but, surprisingly enough, he found that mercury worked best.)

b) Then he turned the tube upside down and placed it in a dish filled with more mercury.*

(***WARNING – HAZARDOUS CHEMICALS**! Don't try this at home, kids. Mercury is horribly poisonous. In large amounts, it can seriously damage your nerves, skin, blood, stomach, liver and kidneys. Tiny amounts are found in the grey stuff used to fill your teeth. So don't do anything to upset your dentist!)

c) Every day, he went to look at the tube and noticed how the level of the mercury rose and fell. This went on for some time.

d) Then he had a brainwave. The mercury went up and down, depending on differences in air pressure.

HIGH PRESSURE PUSHING DOWN ON THE MERCURY IN THE DISH MADE THE MERCURY IN THE TUBE RISE. LOW PRESSURE MADE IT FALL.

Bet you wouldn't have thought of that!

Did timid old Torricelli brag about his discovery? No way. He liked to keep himself to himself. Besides, he was much more interested in maths than meteorology. Very odd. Instead, he scribbled a note, which read:

> *We live submerged at the bottom of an ocean of elementary air, which is known by incontestable experiments to have weight.*

This basically means "We live at the bottom of the atmosphere. And we've worked out that it's heavy." Then Torricelli flung his note into a dusty drawer and forgot all about it.

3 Luckily, other people blew Torricelli's trumpet for him. Later, a brilliant French scientist, Blaise Pascal (1623–1662), tried to improve on Torricelli's barometer. He persuaded his brother-in-law to climb up a local (and, luckily, extinct) volcano to try his new invention out. Oh, and to test his latest theory that air pressure drops the higher you go because there's less air pressing down on you.

Of course, lazy Blaise didn't go up the mountain with him. He was under enough pressure already. But he arranged for some monks to witness the experiment and vouch that it was carried out fair and square. And it turned out that he was right. The higher you go, the weaker the air pressure.

4 Some time later, poor Pascal fell ill from overwork and his doctor ordered him to rest. Guess what he did for relaxation? He wrote an essay on air pressure! Still, it made him feel better, so who's complaining? Perhaps you could try this next time you're feeling off colour?

5 In honour of Pascal, pressure is sometimes measured in units called, rather boringly, 'Pascals'. Actually, it's measured in hectopascals (1 hectopascal = 100 pascals). Normal air pressure is 1013.2 hectopascals.

6 Remember good old Otto von Guerike? He was the first person to use a barometer to forecast the weather when he predicted that a sharp fall in pressure meant there would be a bad storm.

7 But you can forget about mercury, or sea water, or honey. There's a much simpler way to make your own barometer. First find a frog, place it in a jar of pond water and cover the top with a cloth. (Make sure the cloth is nice and holey so that your barometer can breathe.)

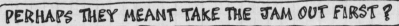
PERHAPS THEY MEANT TAKE THE JAM OUT FIRST?

Now wait ... and listen carefully.

How to read your frogometer:

• If your frog croaks a lot, pressure is falling with stormy weather on its way. (Remember, low pressure means unsettled weather.)

• If your frog croaks a bit, pressure is rising so

expect a fine spell. (Remember, high pressure means good weather.)

• If your frog stops croaking altogether, get yourself a new frog.

(Remember to put the frogs back in their pond afterwards.)

I THINK YOUR FROG'S CROAKED IT!

Earth-shattering fact

If you're up a mountain and fancy a panful of pasta for lunch, cook it for longer than it says on the packet. Why? Well, air pressure changes the temperature at which water boils. The higher you go, the lower the pressure and the lower the boiling point. So, the water comes to the boil more quickly, but the food takes longer to cook.

Masses of air

The air in the awesome atmosphere never stays still. It's always on the move, shunted and shoved by changes in pressure and temperature. The way all this air moves from day to day is what makes our daily weather.

Air masses are enormous clumps of air which form over land and sea. They can be warm, cold, dry or wet, depending on where they come from: coming from a hot desert, the air mass would be hot and dry, but if it forms over a cold sea it would be cold and damp. You can't see them but they're always there, drifting slowly around the Earth. They're pushed along by the winds and help to spread the sun's heat around. Some air masses are horribly huge. One was estimated to be about the size of the country of Egypt. Wow!

Back to the front

Being an air mass is a bit like being a dodgem car. One minute, you're drifting along happily, minding your own business. The next, you've bumped into another air mass which wants to shove you out of the way. All you can do is shove back.

The point where two squabbling air masses meet is called a front. The weather here can be very unsettled. Fronts come in three varieties – cold, warm and occluded. Try impressing your teacher with this tricky technical term. An occluded front is one that's formed when a cold front overtakes a warm front. But it's cunning cold fronts that cause stormy weather. Here's how a cold front is born:

1 A cold air mass meets a warm air mass.

2 The cold air cuts under the warm air, forcing it upwards.

3 The warm air rises quickly and sharply, making storm clouds and rain.

4 Along some cold fronts, the moving air causes rows of squally storms that can stretch on for up to 800 kilometres.

Highs and lows

MONA'S NOTES:

Just to keep you on your toes, air pressure is different all over the world. Why? Because the sun heats up some places more than others. The rule is that cold air is heavy, so it sinks and causes high pressure. Warm air is light, so it rises and causes low pressure. Got that? Just like you and me, the atmosphere has its highs and lows.

A high is a spiralling area of high pressure. The highest pressure is in the middle. And the good news is that highs usually bring settled, sunny, dry weather and clear blue skies. Hurray!

SPIRALLING HIGH PRESSURE

EARTH

BIRD'S-EYE VIEW

HIGHEST PRESSURE

NICE SUNNY, DRY WEATHER

EARTH

A low, on the other hand, means it's time to get your brolly out. This is a spiralling area of low pressure. The lowest pressure is in the centre. The bad news is that lows usually bring cloudy, wet weather and stormy skies. (You could impress your teacher by calling this a cyclone or a depression - sounds like quite a good name for a low!)

Here's a simple experiment to find the nearest low to you.

Ready?

1. Stand outside with your back to the wind.
2. Now, where do you live? Are you in the northen hemisphere? In this case your nearest low is on your left - because winds in the north blow anti-clockwise around a low.

YOU

LOW

NORTH POLE

WIND

EARTH

3. But if you live in the southern hemisphere, it's the other way round. The nearest low is on your right - because winds in the south blow clockwise.

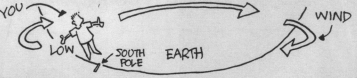

YOU

LOW

SOUTH POLE

EARTH

WIND

Don't worry if all this pressure's really getting to you. The awesome atmosphere is horribly hard to follow. It's also horribly unstable. It just can't sit still for a minute. Know the feeling? And this is what makes for stormy weather. But all this talk of highs and lows is just the beginning. Get ready for a very rough ride…

WILD, WET AND WINDY

Imagine you're lounging about in the garden on a hot summer's day. The sun's out, the sky's blue, and your mum's just bought you a long, cold drink. Lovely! Don't be fooled. This is weather on its best behaviour. But things can quickly change for the worse. And there's nothing nastier in nature than a savage storm. Behind every storm, there are sinister storm clouds and buckets of rain. And the incredible, invisible force of the wind. You can't see it, but it certainly knows how to blow.

A question of wind...

We thought Mona was in need of a challenge, so we sent her off on a mission – to tackle class 5C's problem with wind...

There isn't much to know about wind, is there? It's just moving air.

Yes, but have you ever thought how it moves in the first place?

Er...no

Well listen to this. It's all down to air pressure — you know, the rule that cold air is heavy and sinks to make high pressure, and warm air is light and rises to make low pressure?

Doesn't make much sense to me.

Ok, imagine your big sister sitting on top of you, squashing you flat. You could say that was high pressure. When you kick her off you get low pressure! See?

If I kicked her off, I'd get a medal!

Oh yeah, but what's it got to do with wind?

Well, air always moves from high to low pressure, and as it moves, hey presto! You've got wind.

Ooooh, Miss!

No, not *that* sort of wind!

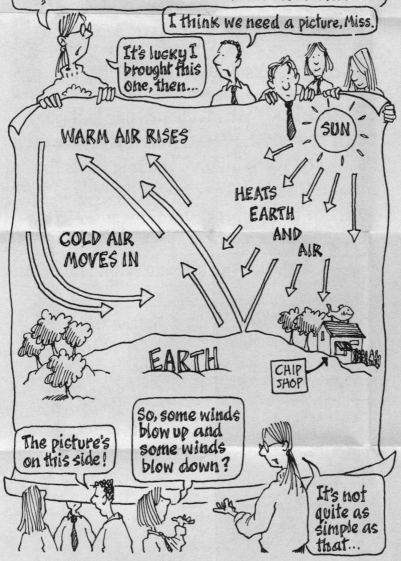

Winds don't blow in a straight line from A to B.

What happens then?

Well the Earth is spinning on its axis.

It's *What*, Miss?

Its axis, that's an imaginary line that runs down its middle. It's spinning all the time, even now, while we're talking. The spin flings the winds sideways. They're flung to the right in the northern hemisphere and flung to the left in the southern hemisphere.

You could call it a "Highwind" fling, Miss!

You *could*. Here's a picture to help explain these two flings.

WINDS

NORTH

← AXIS

EARTH

EARTH'S ROTATION

← WINDS

SOUTH

Once these flings are flung are they far flung flings?

So do winds just blow all over the place?

Good question! Nope!

54

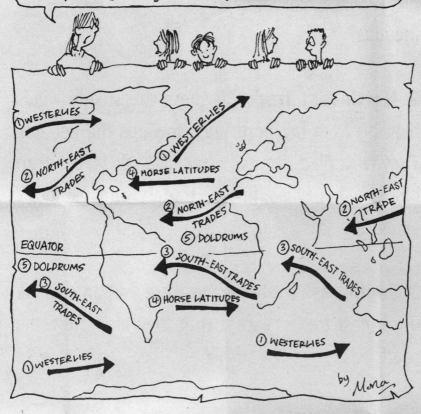

They aren't just flung about willy nilly. They blow around the world in fixed patterns. Here's a map I've put together to prove it:

1. WESTERLIES
2. NORTH-EAST TRADES
1. WESTERLIES
4. HORSE LATITUDES
2. NORTH-EAST TRADES
2. NORTH-EAST TRADE
5. DOLDRUMS
EQUATOR
5. DOLDRUMS
3. SOUTH-EAST TRADES
3. SOUTH-EAST TRADES
3. SOUTH-EAST TRADES
4. HORSE LATITUDES
1. WESTERLIES
1. WESTERLIES

by Mona

1 Westerlies – winds blowing from the west. Winds are always named after the direction they

55

are blowing from. So, a westerly blows from the west, an easterly blows from the east – get the idea?

2 North-east trades – these are steady winds blowing from the north-east towards the equator. They're called 'trades' because they used to blow sailing ships full of traders and explorers across the seas.

3 South-east trades – these are the same as the north-east trades, except that they blow from the south-east.

4 Horse latitudes – an area of very, very light winds. In the past, when sailing ships ruled the seas, woe betide any that got stuck here. They could be stranded for days. Often there was only one way out. They had to chuck the horses they carried overboard to make the ships a bit lighter just in case a bit of a breeze blew up.

Doldrums — an area of dead calm at the equator where there's no wind and nothing moves for days on end. No wonder sailors caught here were said to be really 'down in the doldrums'.

Equator – it doesn't really exist! It's an imaginary line around the Earth exactly half way between the Poles.

Earth-shattering fact

The highwind fling does have a proper, but more boring name. It's called the Coriolis force, after French scientist, Gustave-Gaspard Coriolis (1792–1843). Gustave was the first person to work out that an invisible force makes objects fly in a curved path rather than in a straight line. He also found that his force causes the spin that can set off hurricanes and tornadoes. Forceful Gust, er ... sorry ... Gustave, set out his theory in a boring paper called:

"ON THE EQUATIONS OF RELATIVE MOTIONS OF SYSTEMS OF BODIES"

It was baffling, but brilliant, seeing as nobody had ever thought of this before. He went on to write a book on billiards. Not quite so brilliant, eh?

Five wild facts about wind!

1 The ancient Greeks thought that the winds were the breath of the gods. There were eight wind gods, one for each wind direction. Let's hope none of them had bad breath.

LET'S HOPE THIS IS THE BREATH OF THE GODS AND NOT OUR DINNER!

Other crackpot Greeks believed wind was made when trees waved their leaves. Weird!

2 Jet streams weren't discovered until the Second World War, when pilots found themselves slowing almost to a stop when they flew against certain winds. Jet streams are super speedy westerly winds that blow high up in the atmosphere. They're very strong, and can race along at up to 500 kilometres per hour, and very long, trailing for almost 4,000 kilometres.

They can also drag lows about, with squally storms following on behind them. The only place on Earth where you can actually feel the jet stream is at the top of Mount Everest and other very high mountains. So why not suggest a special geography field trip?

3 The good news is, jet streams can speed planes on their way – well, they can if you happen to be flying from New York to London. Then the wind is behind you, speeding your plane along. The bad news is, flying back again takes about an hour longer because you're flying against the wind.

4 Overall, the windiest place in the world is blowy Commonwealth Bay in Antarctica, where gales gust at speeds of 320 kilometres per hour – as fast as a racing car. But the ghastliest gust of wind ever recorded blew at 408 kilometres per hour, on Barrow Island, off the north-west coast of Australia.

5 If you think that's bad, thank your lucky stars you don't live on planet Neptune. There winds can howl at a mind-boggling 2,000 kilometres per hour. Now that's really wild!

Depending on where you live in the world, you might have your own local wind. If you live in Germany, for example, your local wind's called the foehn. It's a warm, dry wind that blows off the mountains in late winter. And it gets blamed for everything. It's said to make people feel headachy, sick, tired, depressed and more irritable than usual. (So that's what's wrong with your geography teacher!) It's even been known to drive folk mad! People make a packet out of selling special necklaces, bracelets and even insoles for your shoes to make you feel better. Talk about blowing things out of all proportion!

Hot and sticky

There's something else lurking in the awesome atmosphere. You can't see it but it's there, all around you, all the time. It's name is … water vapour. It's actually water in gas form. And this invisible vapour's vital to the weather. Without it, you wouldn't have clouds, rain or snow. Imagine that, what would geography teachers have to talk about? The amount of water vapour in the air is called humidity. It changes from place to place. Warm air can hold more water than cold air. That's why you get hot and sticky on holiday. It's horrible humidity that makes you sweat like a pig. (You sweat a lot when it's hot and dry too but in humid air the sweat doesn't dry off you so quickly.) Nice!

Apart from how much you sweat, there are other ways of measuring horrible humidity. You could use a hygrometer. (That's the tricky technical term for a machine that measures wetness.) The first hygrometer was built by Swiss whizz, Horace Bénédict de Saussure in 1783. A keen explorer, hearty Horace got most of his best ideas when he was halfway up a mountain. Horace's hygrometer used a human hair to measure humidity. So how did it work? And what do you think happened when Horace stuck his hair hygrometer outside on a nice, humid day? Did it…

a) shrink in size?

b) grow longer?

c) stay exactly the same?

HUMAN HAIR

ANSWER

b) Hair-raising Horace Bénédict discovered that human hair expands or stretches when it soaks up water from the air. This means humidity is high. Hair shrinks when the air is dry and humidity is low.

HIGH HUMIDITY LOW HUMIDITY BALD

Storm clouds gathering

But what on Earth has water vapour got to do with stormy weather? The simple answer is clouds. Not just the fluffy, white, puffy ones that float gently past your window but glowering, grey storm clouds, the meanest, nastiest clouds in the sky.

Clouds form when:

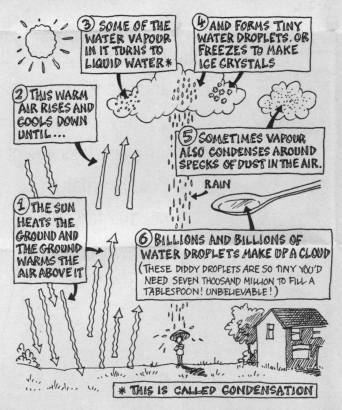

③ SOME OF THE WATER VAPOUR IN IT TURNS TO LIQUID WATER *

④ AND FORMS TINY WATER DROPLETS, OR FREEZES TO MAKE ICE CRYSTALS

② THIS WARM AIR RISES AND COOLS DOWN UNTIL...

⑤ SOMETIMES VAPOUR ALSO CONDENSES AROUND SPECKS OF DUST IN THE AIR.

RAIN

① THE SUN HEATS THE GROUND AND THE GROUND WARMS THE AIR ABOVE IT

⑥ BILLIONS AND BILLIONS OF WATER DROPLETS MAKE UP A CLOUD (THESE DIDDY DROPLETS ARE SO TINY YOU'D NEED SEVEN THOUSAND MILLION TO FILL A TABLESPOON! UNBELIEVABLE!)

* THIS IS CALLED CONDENSATION

DIY weather forecast

Weather forecasting – it's all in a day's work for Mona the meteorologist, but you could have a go too. First you'll need to get matey with a few clouds. Your teacher will probably tell you there are ten types of clouds. Don't listen. Unless you want to be a serious meteorologist, you can easily cheat a bit. All you need to know are the three main groups listed here and the types of weather they bring. So here goes, let's see if you could make it as a weather forecaster:

IF YOU SEE WHITE, PUFFY CLOUDS FLOATING ABOVE YOU, WITH A SORT OF CAULIFLOWER SHAPE TO THEM, YOU CAN BET YOUR LIFE THEY'RE **CUMULUS** CLOUDS. IF THEY'RE SMALL AND HIGH UP ABOVE THE GROUND, THEY'RE FRIENDLY, AND BRING GOOD WEATHER, BUT AS THEY GET BIGGER THEY MIGHT BRING SHOWERS.

A

CUMULUS

B

STRATUS

GOT A LOW-LYING LAYER OR SHEET OF CLOUD HANGING ABOUT? YOU CAN CALL IT **STRATUS**. IF IT'S CLOSE TO THE GROUND THAT'S BAD NEWS, YOU COULD BE IN FOR SOME FOG AND DRIZZLE.

69

CIRRUS

THOSE FEATHERY WISPY BITS OF CLOUD YOU SOMETIMES SEE WAY UP ABOVE YOU ARE CALLED **CIRRUS CLOUDS,...**

...AND THEY'RE MORE BAD NEWS, I'M AFRAID. THERE'S A LOW APPROACHING, SO BAD WEATHER TO COME.

So, stick your head out of the window, and see what you can spot, and if your teacher complains, try saying, "But Miss, I was studying the altocumulus lenticularis."*

* ROUGHLY TRANSLATED, YOU'VE GOT YOUR HEAD IN THE CLOUDS. TO BE PRECISE, YOU'VE GOT YOUR HEAD IN THE LENS—SHAPED (OR OVAL) HIGH CUMULUS CLOUDS SOMETIMES MISTAKEN FOR FLYING SAUCERS! HONESTLY. THEY'RE QUITE RARE, BUT CAN BE DANGEROUS, ESPECIALLY IF YOU'RE A PILOT, AS THEY BRING STRONG, GUSTY WINDS.

The person to blame for all these fancy names was an English chemist and part-time meteorologist, Luke Howard.

I name this cloud...

One cloudy day in 1802, Luke Howard was probably not too hard at work in his chemist's shop. Business was slow. As the day's only customer left the shop, clutching her parcel of pills and potions, Luke found himself staring out of the window, his head in the clouds. And he got so carried away with his day-dreaming that he started giving the clouds names. Not ordinary names like Ben or Samantha but fancy-sounding Latin names like cumulus, stratus and cirrus.

The names sounded seriously scientific but what on Earth did they mean? Any guesses? Prepare to be seriously unimpressed. They just mean 'lumpy heap', 'layer' and 'curly hair', and they simply describe the shapes they make. But Luke was very pleased with his names and it certainly made time pass more quickly. Amazingly, no one had ever thought of naming clouds before. But the idea quickly caught on.

Luke soon became a bit of a star. He was invited to give important lectures and talks to learned scientific societies. First stop was his own local scientific society in London. The audience clapped politely as Luke strode into the room. He bowed and cleared his throat. Then he began:

Ladies and gentlemen, the ocean of air in which we live and move, in which the bolt of heaven is forged, and the fructifying rain condensed, can never be to the zealous Naturalist a subject of tame and unfeeling contemplation... blah, blah, blah...

Of course, nobody understood a word he said. If only he'd stuck to plain English.

*That's the posh word for cloudy. It can also mean 'vague' and 'formless'.

But lucky Luke had the last laugh. In serious scientific circles, his cloud classification was greatly admired. A German poet even wrote a poem about it! And the classification proved so successful it's still used to describe clouds today, not only in Britain but all over the world. Clouds are horribly useful clues to forecasting the weather. For example, one of the first signs that a thunderstorm is coming round the corner is a giant cumulonimbus cloud.

Towering thunderclouds

There's no mistaking a cumulonimbus.* Nimbus is Latin for rain, and when this sky-scraping super-cloud rears its ugly head, you know it's time to take cover. Mount Everest, eat your heart out. These billowing beauties can tower twice as high as titchy old Everest. They're mean, moody, and they mean business. It's in these monster cloud factories that thunderstorms and tornadoes are born.

*Impress your teacher by calling them by their geographical name 'Cbs'– that's what geographers call them for short. And 'cumulonimbus' is a bit of a mouthful.

An hour in the life of a thundercloud

Thunderclouds grow in warm, moist air. That's why thunderstorms are common on summer afternoons. Lots of air holding lots of water vapour rises very quickly and condenses. Then the cloud billows up, and up, and up...

A fully-fledged thundercloud can hold half a million tonnes of water. That's an awful lot of rain. What happens is this. As water droplets, snowflakes and ice crystals whirl about inside the cloud, they bump and bash into each other, and grow bigger and bigger until they're too heavy to hang around any longer. Then they fall to the ground. If the air is warm near the ground all the snow and ice melts into rain. If the air is really cold then it will fall as ice and snow and you might get a day off school, hooray!

Many people think that raindrops are tear-shaped. Wrong! They're shaped like circles with the bottoms cut off. Officially a raindrop is about 1.5 millimetres across – which is...

THIS BIG ➞ ☼

Anything smaller counts as drizzle. But some raindrops grow to the size of peas. Pretty big, eh?

THAT'S THIS BIG ➡

Ever heard the saying "saving up for a rainy day"? Well, for people living near Mount Wai-'ale-'ale in Hawaii, almost every day's a rainy day. It rains for about 335 days of the year, that's a soaking wet 11 metres of rain a year. So don't go to Hawaii if you want to save money!

The rain you see splattering against the window pane has fallen millions of times before. In the water cycle, it's recycled again and again. The sun heats the oceans and millions of litres of water evaporate and rise into the air as water vapour. As it rises, it cools and condenses into liquid water. This falls as rain into rivers which carry it back to the sea. Then the whole thing begins again. So the rain that falls today, may already have soaked the Ancient Romans or drenched the long-dead dinosaurs!

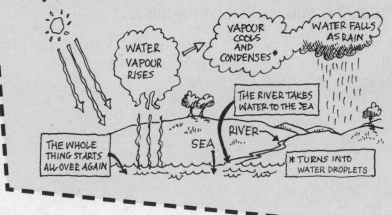

From invisible water vapour to towering thunderclouds and torrential rain, the weather is full of horrible

surprises. A thunderstorm can strike like a bolt from the blue. Could you stand the heat? Get ready to watch some wild weather fireworks…

RUMBLING THUNDER

D id you know that at any time of any day there are thousands of thunderstorms brewing on Earth? And there could be one near you! If there is, watch out for a sizzling spectacle. Gasp as the sky turns purply black with terrible, towering thunderclouds. Tremble as the fireworks really begin. Scream (with horror or delight – you choose) as a dazzling flash of lightning is swiftly followed by a deafening rumble of thunder. CRASH! BANG! WALLOP! And it's all over ... or is it? Look out, the whole thing is starting again!

But, hang on a minute, what on Earth is a thunderstorm? Are you sure you're brave enough to find out?

Six rumbling facts about thunderstorms

1 Thunderstorms happen when damp air near the Earth's surface is warmed by the sun and starts to rise. Thunderstorms happen nearly every day in some tropical parts of the world. As the warm air rises, it cools and condenses and creates gigantic cumulonimbus clouds (see page 75).

2 Other storms start along cold fronts when cool air forces warm air upwards. They grow in a row called a squall line. Sometimes the storm at the end of the row gets stronger and stronger. These storms are called 'supercells' and are the biggest thunderstorms. They often bring a friend along, too – a tornado!

COLD AIR UNDERCUTS THE WARM AIR

COLD AIR

WARM AIR RISES FORMING STORM CLOUDS

3 If you want to have a go at a bit of weather forecasting, wait for the next thunderstorm. Then tell everyone not to worry, it'll be over in 30 minutes. You'll probably be right, most thunderstorms quickly run out of steam.

4 Thunderstorms are packed with energy. Enough to power the whole USA for 20 minutes. And if you think that every day there are about 45,000 thunderstorms raging around the world, that's an awesome amount of energy. There are at least 2,000 storms simmering away as you read this book!

5 What goes up must come down. In a thundercloud, rising air has to fall eventually, and this causes strong downbursts of air called 'microbursts'. They drag torrential rain down with them. Worse still, when a murderous microburst hits the ground, it smashes outwards, causing winds of up to 160 kilometres per hour. Particularly perilous for planes. In 1982, a microburst knocked a plane clean out of the sky as it took off from New Orleans, USA. And there's no easy way of telling when or where one will strike.

6 As a thundercloud sucks up warm air, wild currents of wind are stirred up inside it. They race up through the cloud so fast, they can rip the wings off a plane. And take pilots for a terrifying ride, as American airman Lt Col William Rankin found out in July 1959. He was flying above the Carolina coast in the USA when the engine of his jet fighter suddenly failed. The plane went out of control and Rankin was forced to bail out ... straight into a thundercloud. Incredibly, he lived to tell the tale:

At first, I didn't know what was happening. It was so quick I didn't really have time to think. All I knew was that I had to get my parachute open. It was easier said than done. By the time it opened, I'd already been beaten black and blue. I found myself in an angry ocean of boiling clouds, all black, grey and white, spilling over each other. The winds inside the cloud were incredible. I was buffeted in all directions, up, down, sideways, over and over. And the darkness ... I couldn't see anything. I didn't want to see anything. I kept my eyes tight shut. It was like being in a cage of wild animals, shrieking and screaming, and beating me with huge sticks, trying to crush me to death. But the rain was the worst thing. Sometimes it fell in such heavy drenching sheets that I

thought I would drown in mid-air.
By some miracle, my parachute
wasn't damaged and I
finally dropped through
the base of the cloud.

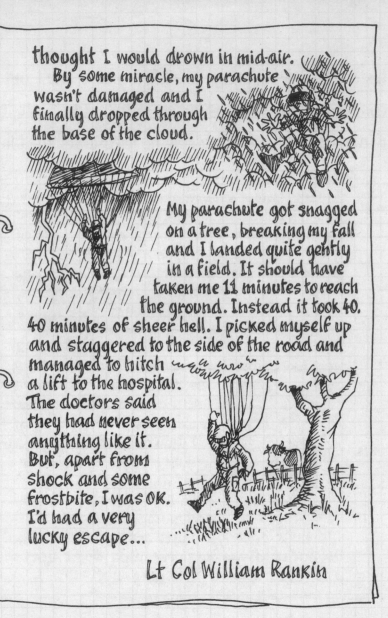

My parachute got snagged
on a tree, breaking my fall
and I landed quite gently
in a field. It should have
taken me 11 minutes to reach
the ground. Instead it took 40.
40 minutes of sheer hell. I picked myself up
and staggered to the side of the road and
managed to hitch
a lift to the hospital.
The doctors said
they had never seen
anything like it.
But, apart from
shock and some
frostbite, I was OK.
I'd had a very
lucky escape...

Lt Col William Rankin

Stormy warning signs

Don't panic, what happened to Lt Col Rankin is very, very rare. The best thing you can do is keep well away from storms. But could you spot a storm approaching? Which of these stormy warning signs do you believe and which are too stupid to be true? You can tell a storm is coming because…

a) You get a splitting headache? True/false?

b) Your hair stands on end? True/false?

c) The clouds turn green? True/false?

d) The milk turns sour? True/false?

ANSWER

a) Possibly true. This could mean a storm is brewing, or that you've been overdoing your geography homework. Some people are very sensitive to the weather and get headaches when the air is damp or full of static electricity – which it is just before a thunderstorm. Other people say they can feel the weather in their bones. Ouch! **b)** Possibly true. But, if this happens, it may already be too late! A lightning strike may be only minutes away. Your hair stands on end because there's so much static electricity in the air. **c)** Possibly true. If the

88

clouds turn slightly green at the bottom, get ready to be hit by a hailstorm. (If your little brother turns green, he's probably about to be sick!) **d)** Definitely false. This is just an old wives' tale. Milk turns sour if you leave it out of the fridge in a warm place and that's got absolutely nothing to do with thunderstorms.

It wasn't just old wives who had funny ideas about thunder. Once upon a time people didn't think thunder was anything to do with weather at all. They thought it was a weapon used by the gods when they were very, very angry. Thunder gets its name from Thor, the Norse thunder god. He was famous for his fiery temper, and made thunder by hurling his huge hammer across the sky.

THUNDERIN' THOR

EARLY MORNING IN ASGARD, HOME OF THE GODS...

In his palace, Thor, the thunder god opened his eyes and stretched. He felt on the table beside his bed. But there was nothing there. His precious hammer had gone...

Thor fell into a thunderous rage...

FIND MY HAMMER! OR ELSE!

RIGHT HO, BOSS, KEEP YOUR HAIR ON!

He reached the castle of the frost giant, Thrym, who'd stolen the hammer.

HAND IT OVER! OR YOU'LL BE SORRY!

Loki turned into a falcon and flew away...

NO WAY! NOT UNTIL I MARRY FREYJA

Freyja was the goddess of love. When she heard that Thrym wanted to marry her she burst into tears...

Trouble was, Thor's Hammer was the god's only weapon against the giants...

BUT HE'S SO UGLY!

I'LL TAKE THAT AS A NO, THEN

I HAVE A CUNNING PLAN, HERE'S WHAT WE'LL DO, BOSS...

I'LL WEAR WHAT?

Instead of Freyja, they dressed Thor in a wedding dress and a veil to hide his beard... GRRRR!

At the wedding feast, Thor ate one whole oxen, eight large salmon and drank three barrels of mead...

HE LOOKS LOVELY

THAT HELMET'S GOT TO GO!

BURP!

THAT'S MY GIRL!

Gormless Thrym didn't suspect a thing...

Then the moment arrived for the wedding presents

I GOT YOU THIS DEAR, I HOPE YOU LIKE IT

Thor threw off his veil and killed Thrym

THAT'LL DO NICELY, NOW I'LL BE OFF!

Then he and Loki set off back to Asgard. (Thor had changed back into his own clothes by then.)

What on Earth is lightning?

As air rushes up and down inside a thundercloud, it has an electrifying effect.

CRASH!

WHOOSH!

CRACKLE!

STATIC ELECTRICITY BUILDS UP

POP!

AIR RUSHES UP AND DOWN

The air makes the water droplets and ice particles inside the cloud crash into each other. All this bumping and bashing builds up a store of static electricity. The flash of lightning you see in a storm streaking across the sky is a giant spark of static electricity. That's the same sort you get when you take your jumper off quickly and it makes your hair crackle and stick up. Here's how lightning flashes:

1 Positive electrical charges build up in the top of the cloud. Negative charges build up in the bottom. The ground is also positively charged.

2 When the difference becomes too great, lightning flashes between the negative and positive charges. Inside a cloud, it's called sheet lightning.

3 Lightning that flashes between the cloud and the ground, then back again is called forked lightning.

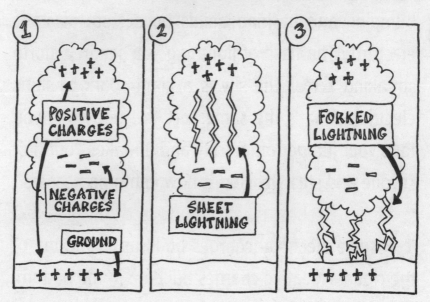

Forked lightning takes the easiest route to the ground. This often means the quickest. Tall trees and buildings are favourite targets. Luckily, most lightning flashes stay safely inside their cloud or leap from one cloud to another. Even so, horrible geographers reckon that about 100 flashes of lightning hit the Earth EVERY SECOND!

When you see lightning, you are also watching the return flash from the ground to the cloud. To your eyes, it looks like a single, long flickering flash. This is because it's travelling so quickly (at lightning fast speeds of up to 140,000 kilometres per second). In fact, there are 30 or more separate flashes racing between the cloud and the ground. Each flash only lasts for a tiny part of a second. Your eyes can just about pick these mini flashes out, which is why the whole thing seems to flicker.

Do you know the saying "lightning never strikes twice"? Well, that's nonsense because it does! The Empire State Building in New York is hit up to 500 times a year. And it's not just buildings that are at risk…

26 June **The Daily Globe** 1977

WAYNESBORO, VIRGINIA, USA
LIGHTNING ROD IN UNLUCKY STRIKE!

Retired national park ranger, Roy C. Sullivan, was today recovering after yet another lucky escape. Yesterday he was struck by lightning … for the seventh time in 35 years. Plucky Roy, 65, is living proof that lightning can strike twice. Roy's totally shocking experiences have earned him the legendary nickname "Lightning Rod". (Well, it's close!) He was first struck in April 1942 when he was working in a fire tower in the park. "Lightning hit the tower seven or eight times," he said. "So I decided to get outta there." He was just a metre or so from the tower when the lightning struck him, burning a strip down his right leg and knocking his big toenail off.

STRIKE ONE

In 1969, Roy had his eyebrows blown off and in 1970, lightning badly burned his left shoulder. He was struck again in 1972 and 1973, and on both occasions his hair caught fire. The second time, the bolt came out of the blue. Lightning threw him clean out of his car and singed both his legs. A strike in 1976 left him with a badly injured ankle.

"You can tell it's coming but it's too late," he explained. "You can smell sulphur in the air, and then your hair will stand up on end, and then it's going to get you. It's like being hit with a sledgehammer. You don't have time to do anything."

The seventh and latest strike happened when Roy was out fishing. "I smelled sulphur and looked up," he told me, "And saw the bolt coming down to get me. Blam! I hope this is the last time. Seven times is enough. In fact, it's too many."

Remarkable Roy knows he is lucky to be alive. No one else has been struck more than three times and survived. Roy takes it all in his stride. When I asked him why the lightning seemed to single him out, Roy shook his head and smiled knowingly. "Some people are allergic to flowers," he said. "I guess I'm just allergic to lightning."

DEADLY ALLERGY

Outwit your teacher

It was lucky that Roy C. Sullivan wasn't keraunophobic (ker-own-oh-phobic). That's the technical term for finding lightning frightening. Dare you steal your teacher's thunder? Put your hand up and say:

Does this mean that you're…

a) scared of thunder?

b) scared of brontosauruses?

c) scared of showing yourself up at football?

And there are plenty of other stormy weather phobias that might make handy excuses. How about ombrophobia (being scared of rain), anemophobia (being scared of wind), chionophobia (being scared of snow) and homichlophobia (being scared of fog)! Got the symptoms for any of these?

EXCUSE ME, MISS, I'M OMBROPHOBIC, ANEMOPHOBIC, CHIONOPHOBIC, AND HOMICHLOPHOBIC!

YOU'RE AN IDIOT!

Note: if you really are brontophobic, you may want to skip the next bit.

What on Earth is thunder?

So should you really be scared of thunder? It certainly makes a lot of noise but it won't do you any harm. But how on Earth does it happen? Here's Mona to explain.

Lightning is hot stuff. It's about five times hotter than the surface of the sun for a start. And as it streaks through the sky, the air in its path heats up to an unbelievably scorching 33,000°C. This makes the air expand at supersonic speed and sends shockwaves shooting through the sky. It's this that makes the booming sound of thunder.

Have you noticed how in a thunderstorm, you see the lightning before you hear the thunder, even though they both happen at exactly the same time? This is because light travels through the air much faster than sound. While lightning zips along at a chaotic 140,000 kilometres per second, sound lags behind at a measly 340 metres per second. Slow coach. Storm round the corner? Try this simple test to guess how far a storm is from your doorstep.

What you need:

- Yourself
- A thunderstorm
- A watch with a second hand

What you do:

1 Wait for a flash of lightning, then look at your watch.

2 Count the seconds until you hear the thunder.

3 Divide the number of seconds by three. This tells you how many kilometres the storm is from you…

SO IF THERE ARE FIVE SECONDS BETWEEN THE LIGHTNING AND THUNDER, THE STORM'S ONLY TWO KILOMETRES AWAY. WATCH OUT! THAT'S PRETTY CLOSE!

Top tips for storm safety

Lightning can be exciting, but watch out, it's also a killer. Around the world, lightning kills hundreds of people (and animals) every year. So if you're caught in a storm, what on Earth can you do? Try to remember these basic Dos and Don'ts and you'll stand a pretty good chance of survival:

Most of these survival tips have something to do with good and bad conductors. No, not the sort that look after orchestras. These are conductors of electricity. Some things are better conductors than others, for example metal and water. This means electricity flows through them easily.

DON'T...

• **Stand under a tall tree.** Lightning always takes the quickest path to the ground so trees and tall buildings are most at risk. The same goes for telephone poles and hill tops (mountaineers, beware!). NEVER stand under a tree in a  storm. Particularly if it's on its own. A direct hit can completely demolish even the toughest tree.

You could even be hit by flying bark exploding off the trunk. This happens when tree sap (a good conductor) expands in the heat. And to make sure it's polished you off completely, the tree might fall on top of you. Timberrrrr!

• **Play a round of golf**. Playing golf can seriously damage your health. Partly because if you're out in the open on a golf course, you're likely to be the tallest thing around – a perfect target for lightning. And metal golf clubs are great conductors. So forget about golf. Unless you live in Arizona, USA. There, a go-ahead golf club has special sensors on the clubhouse roof. These can detect lightning up to 48 kilometres away. Then a siren sounds to warn the golfers.

• **Go fishing with your dad**. Remember Roy 'lightning rod' Sullivan? Twice as many anglers are struck by lightning as golfers because many use long carbon-fibre poles which are excellent conductors. Whatever you do, don't jump into the river. Swimmers are, ahem, sitting ducks for lightning because water's another brilliant conductor.

• **Become a bell ringer**. In the olden days people thought you could scare off lightning by ringing the church bells at it. (Ask your teacher if she remembers that far back.) Ding! Dong! Zap! Their plan backfired … very badly. The lethal combination of being in a tall church steeple and ringing a metal bell meant many batty bell-ringers ended up being fried.

• **Phone a friend**. If you're chatting on the landline and lightning strikes nearby, you could be in for a nasty shock. The lightning could send a killer charge through your telephone line. It's best not to use the phone in a storm and to stay clear of other electrical equipment like computers and TVs. Each year, in the USA, hundreds of TV sets are blown up when lightning hits the outside aerial and passes inside the house. And about 28 people are killed on the phone.

DO...

• **Crouch down on the ground**. Being outside in a storm is full of risks. Most strikes happen in open places such as parks or fields. If you are caught in an open space, crouch down low with your feet together and your hands on your knees. This will make you less of a target. Don't lie down flat.

The wet ground might be a good conductor.

• **Wear your wellies**. Being outside is full of danger (see above). But wearing wellington boots is a good move. Wellies are made of rubber which is a poor conductor of electricity. They block the lightning's path to the ground so it goes another way. Without even lightly toasting your toes.

• **Sit in a car**. Sitting tight in your car is a pretty safe bet. The lightning runs around the car's metal body and into its rubber tyres. Leaving you well alone.

• **Fly in an aeroplane**. If you're in a plane and lightning strikes, you could be in for a bumpy ride. But you'll be quite safe. Like a car, the plane has a metal body which conducts the current around you. Before a plane even takes to the skies, it's zapped with fake lightning in a lab. Just to make absolutely sure it's safe. There's even special lightning-proof shielding around all the gadgets in the cockpit.

- **Stay at home**. This is the safest place to be by far. If you really want to be as safe as houses, stay indoors and watch the storm from the comfort of your armchair…

Safe as houses

Sadly, there's no sure-fire guarantee you'll be completely safe indoors (though its always safer than being outside). But one man's brainwave has made it safer. He was none other than American, Benjamin Franklin, journalist, inventor, politician, poet, and scientist extraordinaire. Sounds impressive, eh? But his family didn't think so. Here's how Benjamin might have tried to impress his doubtful dad with a letter about his shock discovery.

Philadelphia, USA
   Summer 1752

Dear Dad,
          I had to write and tell you about
my latest absolutely brilliant idea. It'll make
you real proud of me, you'll see. Now pay
attention, this is how it all came about.
    Most folks would say we've had an awful
summer. The weather's been wicked for weeks
and weeks. Rain? Huh, I can't think of a day
lately when it hasn't poured. Most people
are really fed up with it. But I've been having
a real good time.

me singing in the rain

    Yesterday we had the
mother of all thunderstorms.
It was fantastically exciting. And the perfect
time to try out my latest experiment. Wait
till you hear this! It's a device for protecting
buildings from lightning strikes.
    Anyway, the storm was at its height and
really raging as I stepped outside with my
kite.

          Don't get me wrong, Dad, this
was no children's picnic game. It was a
serious experiment and the kite was my
most perfect tool. I attached it to a long

                              P.T.O ...

111

piece of wire and fixed a key to the end.
I wanted to attract the
lightning into the key. Yeah, I
know it was dangerous, but
I knew if I could just get this
right, wow, even you would
say it was worth it.

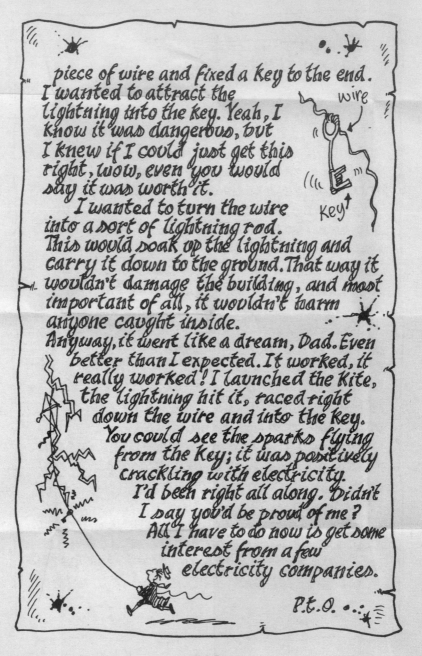

wire

Key

I wanted to turn the wire
into a sort of lightning rod.
This would soak up the lightning and
carry it down to the ground. That way it
wouldn't damage the building, and most
important of all, it wouldn't harm
anyone caught inside.
Anyway, it went like a dream, Dad. Even
better than I expected. It worked, it
really worked! I launched the kite,
the lightning hit it, raced right
down the wire and into the key.
You could see the sparks flying
from the key; it was positively
crackling with electricity.
I'd been right all along. Didn't
I say you'd be proud of me?
All I have to do now is get some
interest from a few
electricity companies.

P.T.O.

112

I know they're gonna love this idea. They won't be able to resist it. It's gonna make me rich. Yippee!

So you see, Dad, I know you think all this science and experimenting and stuff is a waste of my time. But how can I give it all up now and come back to the family firm? Soap making just isn't for me, Dad. But at least now you can see I'm serious about science.

Gotta go now. A man's just called to see if I can make him a portable rod for his umbrella.

Write soon and let me know what you think?

Your son

Ben

If you live in a very tall house or block of flats, you've probably got a lightning conductor on your building. See if you can spot it. Look out for a copper strip running down the outside of the building. Look up and you might see where the strip is attached to a metal rod that's fixed to the highest point on the roof.

What the hail is it?

Meanwhile, you've been deafened by thunder and fried by lightning, and it isn't over yet – the thunderstorm has one more surprise in store. Picture the scene. You're soaked to the skin and starting to look like a drowned rat when ... suddenly what feels like a lorry-load of rock-hard hailstones starts bashing you on the head.

Phew! The best thing for it is to put your feet up in front of the fire while you thaw out and find out what the hail is hail.

1 Hailstones are born in thunderclouds when ice crystals are tossed up and down. Each time, a layer of water freezes on to the crystal. When it's heavy enough, it falls as hail. If you cut a hailstone in half, it looks like an icy onion, with alternate layers of clear and frosty ice.

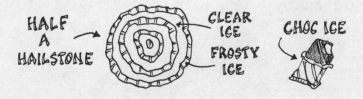

HALF A HAILSTONE — CLEAR ICE FROSTY ICE — CHOC ICE

2 Five German pilots knew just what an ice crystal goes through. In 1930, they bailed out of their aircraft into a thundercloud. Only to become the centres of human hailstones. Coated in layers of ice, they finally fell frozen to the ground. Tragically, four pilots died. It was a miracle that even one pilot survived.

3 The pilots weren't the only living things to fall in hail. In 1894 in a hailstorm in the USA, a gopher turtle as big as a brick fell to Earth as a hailstone. It too had been bounced up and down and covered in ice. No one knows how the turtle got there.

4 Hang on to your hard hat if you're caught in a hailstorm. Hailstones are more or less pea-sized, and weigh less than a gramme but they can grow as big and heavy as oranges. Which is nothing compared to...

5 ...a hailstone the size of a watermelon, which fell in Coffeyville, Kansas, USA in September 1970, or the football-sized hailstone that fell in Aurora, Nebraska in 2003.

6 Most hailstorms last for less than ten minutes but they can cause millions of pounds of damage. They smash roofs and windows, shatter car windscreens, strip the leaves from trees and totally flatten farmers' crops, snapping plant stems as thick as your thumbs. In America, the problem's so serious that farmers take out special hail insurance.

Lightning, thunder, rain, hail and frozen turtles… Whatever will the weather do next? But these aren't the only things to fall from thunderclouds. Are you brave enough to go storming into the next chapter, where you can really get yourself into a spin with a terrifying tornado, some of the stormiest weather of all?

TERRIBLE TWISTERS

What spins like a top, roars like a lion and can blow a house to pieces? This might sound just like your teacher in a temper, but the correct answer is a terrible twister or tornado. A tornado is a horribly violent funnel-shaped storm which spins down from a thundercloud. If a tornado starts to do the twist near you, don't stick around to watch. It'll tear apart everything in its path. Trouble is, you can never tell where a terrible twister will strike next...

What on Earth is a tornado?

In weather, one thing always leads to another. Remember supercell thunderstorms? The ones that grow along cold fronts? They're where tornadoes are born. Geographers don't know exactly what makes tornadoes tick. But they can guess. Are you brave enough to find out how a tornado grows?

Let's twist again

1 Inside the thundercloud air starts to spin. No one knows exactly why. Down below the ground warms the air.

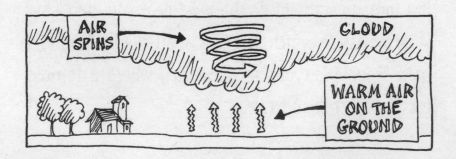

2 As the air spins, it stretches down towards the warmer air near the ground. It also begins to spin faster.

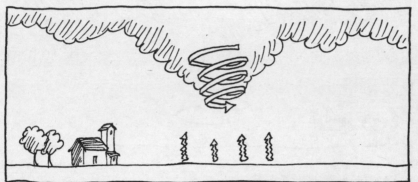

3 This spinning sucks warm air up from the ground.

SUCKED UP WARM AIR

4 As the warm air rises, it cools and condenses to form a whirling funnel-shaped cloud.

5 The cloud looks like an elephant's trunk hanging down from the thundercloud.

6 When it touches the ground, it's a tornado. And then it's off…

THUNDERCLOUD

DOWN DRAFT

TORNADO GOES THIS WAY

SPINNING FUNNEL

HOUSE GOES THIS WAY

UP DRAFT

Tornadoes spin anticlockwise to the north of the equator and clockwise to the south. Usually!

Tornado teasers

Want to know more about terrible twisters but in too much of a spin to ask? Time to call an expert in. Here's Mona, ace meteorologist, to take off some of the pressure.

IT VARIES. MOST PROBABLY TRAVEL QUITE A BIT FASTER THAN YOU CAN WALK—YOU CAN GET UP TO ABOUT 6.5 KM PER HOUR TOPS—THEY MIGHT REACH 32 KM PER HOUR. SOME HARDLY MOVE AT ALL. BUT OTHERS REALLY ZOOM ALONG AT 115 KM AN HOUR, LIKE A FAIRLY FAST CAR.

I CAN OUTWALK THIS

ON YOUR OWN!

FASTER!

SO HOW LONG DO THEY LAST?

MOST TORNADOES ARE FIVE-MINUTE WONDERS, BUT THEY CAN LAST ANYTHING FROM A SECOND OR TWO TO SEVERAL HOURS. ONCE THEY RUN OUT OF WARM AIR, THEY START TO COLLAPSE. THE LONGEST TORNADO EVER RECORDED LASTED THREE AND A HALF HOURS.

125

PHEW, THAT MUST HAVE BEEN NASTY. IS THERE ALWAYS JUST THE ONE TO WORRY ABOUT?

OH, NO, NOT ALWAYS. IF YOU WERE REALLY UNLUCKY YOU COULD COME ACROSS A WHOLE TORRENT OF TORNADOES- THEY SOMETIMES TRAVEL IN GROUPS UP TO 40 STRONG. COME FACE TO FACE WITH ONE OF THESE GANGS AND YOUR FEET WON'T TOUCH THE GROUND. VERY VIOLENT TORNADOES TEND TO TRAVEL ALONE, BUT SOME TOW ALONG A FEW MINI-TWISTERS. THESE ARE MUCH SMALLER FUNNELS AND THEY DON'T LAST LONG, BUT YOU'VE STILL GOT TO WATCH THEM. THEY'RE THE ONES THAT WHIP UP THE STRONGEST WINDS.

TORNADOES SOUND PRETTY EXCITING. WHERE CAN I GO TO CATCH ONE?

THEY ACTUALLY HAPPEN ALL OVER THE PLACE, EVEN BRITAIN HAS UP TO 60 A YEAR. BUT THEY'RE BORINGLY SMALL COMPARED TO THE REAL GIANTS. IF YOU WANT TO CATCH SOME OF THE ROUGHEST, TOUGHEST, TWISTIEST TORNADOES, YOU'D HAVE TO HEAD FOR TORNADO ALLEY, THAT'S A STRETCH OF AMERICA RUNNING NORTH FROM TEXAS... CHECK OUT THIS MAP...

126

WELL, IF YOU'RE COMPLETELY MAD, TORNADO ALLEY GETS HIT MAINLY IN SPRING AND EARLY SUMMER - THAT'S THE TIME OF YEAR MOST PEOPLE LIVING THERE WILL BE PACKING THEIR BAGS AND POPPING OFF TO VISIT A LONG-LOST AUNTIE (ALTHOUGH PREFERABLY NOT ONE IN AUSTRALIA, WHERE THE TORNADO SEASON LASTS FROM NOVEMBER TO MAY) FUNNILY ENOUGH, MOST TORNADOES TURN UP BETWEEN 3 AND 9 P.M.

AND DO THEY DESTROY EVERYTHING THEY COME ACROSS?

SORT OF. WHEN A TORNADO TOUCHES DOWN IT PULVERIZES EVERYTHING IN ITS PATH. IT FLINGS CARS ABOUT, SMASHES HOUSES TO SMITHEREENS AND TURNS FLYING BITS AND PIECES INTO DEADLY WEAPONS. BUT TORNADOES ARE CHOOSY. SOUNDS WEIRD, BUT THEY ACTUALLY HOP ALONG THE GROUND. THIS MEANS THEY MIGHT DECIDE TO SMASH UP YOUR HOUSE BUT SKIP YOUR NEIGHBOUR'S!

YAWN!

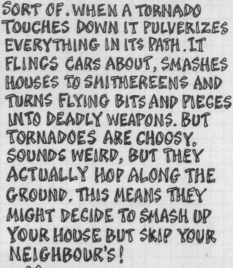

BLIMEY! WHAT MUST IT SOUND LIKE WHEN YOU'RE RIGHT IN THE THICK OF IT?

EAR-WITNESSES DESCRIBE THE NOISE AS A DEAFENING ROAR, LIKE AN EXPRESS TRAIN OR JET PLANE SPEEDING RIGHT PAST YOUR DOOR. OR A SERIOUSLY EAR-SPLITTING SCREAM. SO LOUD YOU CAN HEAR IT UP TO 40 KM AWAY.

128

The speech bubbles in the image:
HMM, MAYBE I'LL STAY AT HOME AFTER ALL.

ACTUALLY, AS THE TORNADO'S TRUNK SWINGS DOWN FROM ITS THUNDERCLOUD, IT MAKES A HORRIBLE SORT OF HISSING SOUND. BUT AS SOON AS IT TOUCHES DOWN, ROOARRRR! THIS WAS A SOUND THAT THE PEOPLE OF JARRELL, A TINY, SLEEPY TOWN IN TEXAS WOULD NEVER FORGET...

28 May *The Daily Globe* 1997

JARRELL TEXAS,

TEXAN TWISTER TEARS TOWN APART

The shocked inhabitants of Jarrell were last night counting the cost of one of the worst tornadoes to hit Texas in the last ten years. The twister, which touched down for barely five minutes, left Jarrell in tatters and 32 people dead. In a town of only 400 people, every survivor knows someone who has been killed.

The tragedy began at 3.15 p.m. when the tornado

hit the ground. One terrified eyewitness saw it approaching. "The sky started to darken," he told our reporter. "Then the funnel started coming through the sky. Everyone panicked. From a distance it looked only a few centimetres tall. Then it covered the whole horizon. As it got closer, bits of buildings were flying around. It was picking up cars and flinging them everywhere. There was a terrible screeching as the trees were mowed down." The tornado blasted a trail of destruction that stretched for 11 kilometres.

TORNADO TROUBLE

The deadly tornado struck almost without warning, taking even the experts by surprise. Meteorologists at the National Weather Service were only able to sound the alarm about half an hour before the tornado touched down. The first Jarrell knew of the on-coming disaster was when the afternoon sky turned black and the funnel appeared with a heart-stopping roar. No one had time to get out of its way.

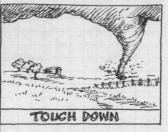
TOUCH DOWN

Of the people killed, many were still in their cars or in the 70 or so houses in the tornado's path. Dozens more have been injured. They are now recovering in hospital. In the fields all round lies the eerie sight of the bodies of cows killed as they grazed. The town itself has been smashed to pieces.

With wind speeds of up to 418 kilometres per hour, the tornado was truly awesome. In fact, it has been officially classified as a Force 5 tornado, the fiercest type there is. County Sheriff, Ed Richards tried to find words to describe the devastation it had caused. "It's like a war zone," he said. "That's all I can say. I don't know how many miles the debris covers." Another stunned survivor, still desperately searching for his missing wife and daughter, said, "My house is gone. Everything's gone."

A rescue operation is now underway, with dogs helping teams of volunteers to search the wreckage. As they pick through the town's flattened remains, hopes of finding survivors are fading. Sheriff Richards again, "We still hope to find somebody alive," he said. "But that would be hoping for a miracle."

Spitting it out

Trashing a town isn't all a tornado is good for. In the centre of tornadoes, pressure plunges to half what it is in the air outside. This pulls warm air up into the funnel and makes it spin faster and faster. (Boring geographers call this spiral a vortex.) As the tornado leapfrogs over land, the vortex sucks up everything in its path, like a gigantic vacuum cleaner. Then it spits it out again. Twisters have terrible table manners.

Not a lot of people know that a tornado can...

Rain cats and dogs. Well, fish and frogs, anyway. When a tornado leaps over lakes or ponds, it can suck up animals from the water, drag them along until it runs out of steam, then dump them on to the ground. Splat! And it's not just slimy fish or frogs. Tornadoes have also sucked up:

Take the train. Everyone's heard of a tornado picking up a car then tossing it away. But in May 1931, a tornado travelling through Minnesota, USA, lifted eight railway carriages clean off the tracks, and dumped them 25 metres away in a ditch. Wow!

Amazingly, only one of the passengers was killed and the locomotive was left on the track.

Move house. In April 1880, a tornado in Missouri, USA, picked up a house and moved it 19 kilometres from home. Another house in Kansas was snatched so sneakily that its owner didn't notice a thing. The first he knew was when he opened the front door and fell 40 metres to the ground. Ouch!

Babysit. In 1981, a tornado twisting through the Italian city of Ancona lifted up a pram with a baby sleeping inside. Then  it put the pram back down on the ground. So gently that the baby didn't feel a thing. Shhh.

 **Pluck a chicken.** Honestly! Some boring geographers put this down to pressure. As the low-pressure tornado passes over the chicken coop, normal air pressure inside the birds' feathers is suddenly much higher than the pressure outside. This makes the feathers explode from their skins!

Others think that the strong winds simply blow the chickens bare. Weird.

Change colour. Most tornadoes are black or dirty grey from all the dust and dirt they suck up from the ground. Red soil turns a tornado red; water vapour turns it white. But pink? A tornado which ripped through Wichita, Kansas, in  April 1991 decided to say it with flowers. It tore through the town's nursery, stocked with geraniums for Mothers' Day. And turned pretty pink with all the petals. Oooh!

Find lost pets. A tornado which struck the town of Sweetwater, Texas, in April 1986 blew a car off the road and smashed its back window. A policeman who went to help the driver noticed a terrified kitten on the back seat. It wasn't the driver's and hadn't been there before the storm. The kitten was later reunited with its delighted owner. Aaah!

Give someone a lift. Imagine being caught right in the middle of a twister? What on Earth would it be like? Not a lot of people look into a tornado and live to tell the tale. One exception was retired army weatherman Roy S. Hall. On 3 May 1948, a tornado struck his home in McKinney, Texas. As the storm raged, the family went to shelter in the bedroom. Seconds later, the outside wall caved in around them. This is how Roy Hall might have described their awful ordeal.

"As the wall caved in, the storm suddenly stopped its dreadful screeching. It was as if I'd put my hands over my ears, blocking out the noise. The only thing I could hear was the thump of my heart beating. The silence was terrible. A strange, blue light lit up the room. Suddenly, I was knocked off my feet and buried under some rubble.
I clawed my way out, grabbed my daughter and waited for my house to blow away. And then I saw it...

   It billowed down from above and hovered there almost completely still. It seemed to spiral out all around us. And I suddenly realized where we were. We were standing right inside the spiral..."

"...right in the middle, trapped inside a real-life tornado! I looked up and saw a shiny wall of cloud about three metres thick all around us. It was like being trapped inside a drainpipe which went up and up, for 100s of metres. And it swayed slightly and tilted over to one side. Down at the bottom, where we were standing, the funnel was about 150 metres wide. The higher up it went, the wider it got. And part of the cloud had a strange shine like a shimmering fluorescent light.

Then just as I thought we were sure to die, I watched the funnel tip over and smash into my neighbour's house. It was horrible. The house blew apart as if it was made of matchsticks. Wood flew everywhere. I really thought we were done for.

But as quickly as it had come, the twister went on its way. We were battered and bruised but at least we were alive."

THE TORNADO CONTINUED ON ITS JOURNEY, HEADING OFF TOWARDS THE SOUTH-EAST. THE FORTUNATE HALL FAMILY ESCAPED ALMOST UNHURT THOUGH THEIR HOME LAY IN RUINS. THEY ALL AGREED THAT IT HAD BEEN A RELATIVELY SMALL PRICE TO PAY...

In 1996, the space probe, SOHO, spotted a giant group of twisters on the sun. Each was as wide as a whole Earth and was spinning at a sensational speed of 54,000 kilometres per hour with gusts of up to 500,000 kilometres per hour. Which makes our titchy Earth twisters look like little pussycats.

A storm in a teacup

So how do the experts decide just how horrible a tornado really is? Here's our very own expert, Mona, to explain.

HMM, MEASURING A TORNADO'S TOUGHNESS IS A TRICKY JOB EVEN FOR A HIGHLY-TRAINED METEOROLOGIST LIKE ME. BUT THERE ARE SOME PRETTY GOOD REASONS WHY.

① NO ONE HAS YET WORKED OUT A FOOLPROOF WAY TO TELL WHEN AND WHERE A TORNADO'S GOING TO STRIKE. SO BEING IN THE RIGHT PLACE AT THE RIGHT TIME IS THE FIRST PROBLEM. AND EVEN IF BY SOME MIRACLE I'VE GOT THERE, WHAT ARE THE CHANCES I'LL HAVE ALL MY EQUIPMENT WITH ME? PRETTY SLIM, I CAN TELL YOU. IT'S FAR TOO HEAVY TO LUG AROUND ALL THE TIME.

② INSIDE THE TORNADO THE WINDS ARE SO STRONG, THAT EVEN IF I DID MANAGE TO BE IN THE RIGHT PLACE AT THE RIGHT TIME, **AND** HAD ALL MY INSTRUMENTS WITH ME, IT'D SMASH THEM ALL TO PIECES ANYWAY.

SO, WHAT CAN I DO? LUCKILY THE FABULOUS FUJITA TORNADO SCALE COMES IN HANDY IN THESE SITUATIONS. IT'S A SIX POINT SCALE THAT GRADES TORNADOES BY THE CHAOS THEY CAUSE, THEN GUESSES THE WIND SPEED ACCORDINGLY. HERE'S HOW IT WORKS...

HOLD ON, I'LL BRING IT CLOSER!

The Enhanced Fjuita Tornado Scale

scale	wind speed	damage
F0	90-130 Km/h	Light
F1	135-175 Km/h	Moderate
F2	180-220 Km/h	Considerable
F3	225-265 Km/h	Severe
F4	270-310 Km/h	Devastating
F5	more than 315 Km/h	Incredible

Turn the page for the damaging details ➡

143

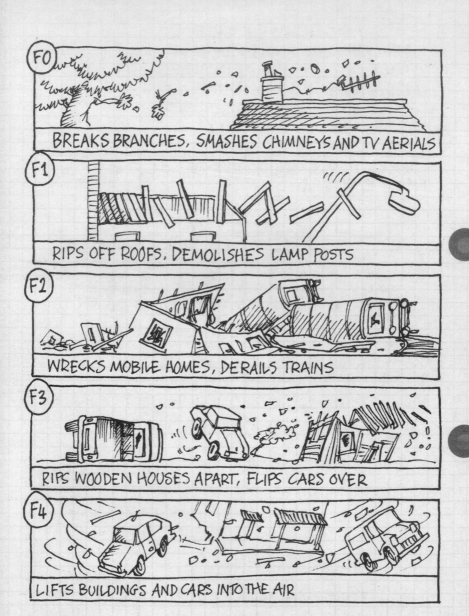

FO — BREAKS BRANCHES, SMASHES CHIMNEYS AND TV AERIALS

F1 — RIPS OFF ROOFS, DEMOLISHES LAMP POSTS

F2 — WRECKS MOBILE HOMES, DERAILS TRAINS

F3 — RIPS WOODEN HOUSES APART, FLIPS CARS OVER

F4 — LIFTS BUILDINGS AND CARS INTO THE AIR

STRONGEST WIND IN THE WORLD, HURLS CARS HUNDREDS OF METRES

The scale was named after Professor Theodore Fujita, 'Mr Tornado' to his friends. Mr T. is mad about tornadoes. So mad he made one in his lab. Why did he do it? Well, poor Professor Fujita had to wait more than 30 years before seeing his first real live tornado. He even had a number plate made for his car with the number TF 0000! Eventually he couldn't wait any longer. So he invented his very

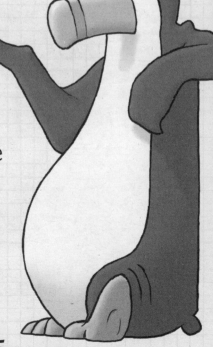

own storm in a teacup. Here's how.

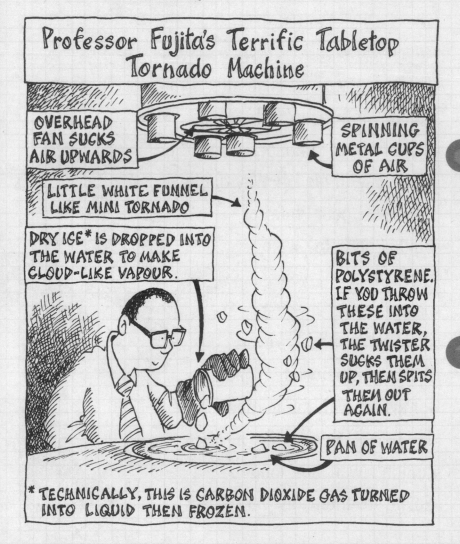

Professor Fujita's Terrific Tabletop Tornado Machine

OVERHEAD FAN SUCKS AIR UPWARDS

SPINNING METAL CUPS OF AIR

LITTLE WHITE FUNNEL LIKE MINI TORNADO

DRY ICE* IS DROPPED INTO THE WATER TO MAKE CLOUD-LIKE VAPOUR.

BITS OF POLYSTYRENE. IF YOU THROW THESE INTO THE WATER, THE TWISTER SUCKS THEM UP, THEN SPITS THEM OUT AGAIN.

PAN OF WATER

* TECHNICALLY, THIS IS CARBON DIOXIDE GAS TURNED INTO LIQUID THEN FROZEN.

Are you brave enough to test a twister?

OK, so most people don't have the luxury of their own tornado lab. So here's another way to do the twist. Actually, there's no need to be scared, it's not that difficult…

What you need:

- a large plastic drinks bottle (empty)
- some water
- a sink

What you do:

1 Half fill the bottle with water. (This bit's easy.)

2 Stand over the sink. (Don't miss this bit out.)

3 Turn the bottle upside down. Then quickly start turning the bottle round in your hands to set the water spinning. (You may need to practise this bit.)

4 Stop turning the bottle.

What happens next?

a) The water pours straight out.

b) The water keeps spinning out in a spiral.

c) Your mum tells you off for missing the sink.

ANSWER

b) Do you know what you've done? You've set a vortex in a spin, and once it's started, it just keeps on spinning. Which is exactly what happens in a tornado.

Could you be a tornado tracker?

Professor Fujita wasn't the only one who longed to see a real-life tornado. Forget football or collecting stamps, some people track twisters for fun! The aim is to find a tornado, drive straight into it and film it without getting hurt or killed. Great! Are you tough enough to try tornado tracking?

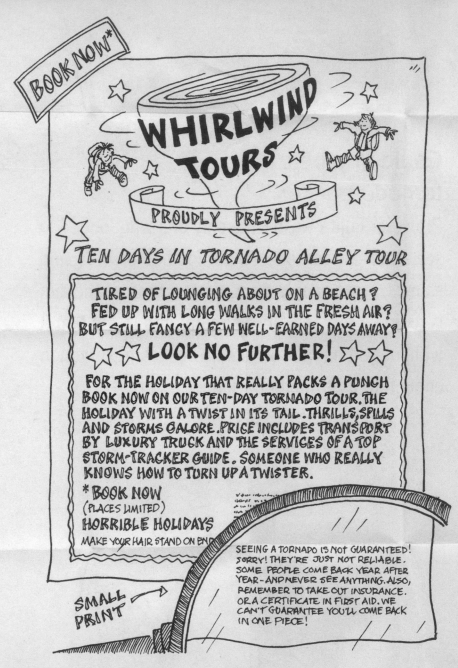

BOOK NOW*

WHIRLWIND TOURS

PROUDLY PRESENTS

TEN DAYS IN TORNADO ALLEY TOUR

TIRED OF LOUNGING ABOUT ON A BEACH?
FED UP WITH LONG WALKS IN THE FRESH AIR?
BUT STILL FANCY A FEW WELL-EARNED DAYS AWAY?

☆ ☆ **LOOK NO FURTHER!** ☆ ☆

FOR THE HOLIDAY THAT REALLY PACKS A PUNCH
BOOK NOW ON OUR TEN-DAY TORNADO TOUR. THE
HOLIDAY WITH A TWIST IN ITS TAIL. THRILLS, SPILLS
AND STORMS GALORE. PRICE INCLUDES TRANSPORT
BY LUXURY TRUCK AND THE SERVICES OF A TOP
STORM-TRACKER GUIDE. SOMEONE WHO REALLY
KNOWS HOW TO TURN UP A TWISTER.

* BOOK NOW
(PLACES LIMITED)
HORRIBLE HOLIDAYS
MAKE YOUR HAIR STAND ON END

SMALL
PRINT →

SEEING A TORNADO IS NOT GUARANTEED!
SORRY! THEY'RE JUST NOT RELIABLE.
SOME PEOPLE COME BACK YEAR AFTER
YEAR - AND NEVER SEE ANYTHING. ALSO,
REMEMBER TO TAKE OUT INSURANCE.
OR A CERTIFICATE IN FIRST AID. WE
CAN'T GUARANTEE YOU'LL COME BACK
IN ONE PIECE!

MONA'S TORNADO TRACKIN' TIPS

WELL I CAN'T SAY I APPROVE OF THE IDEA, BUT IF I REALLY CAN'T STOP YOU GOING OFF ON ONE OF THESE FOOLHARDY ADVENTURES, I'D RATHER YOU WENT PREPARED. THESE TIPS JUST MIGHT HELP YOU TO SEE A TORNADO BEFORE THE TORNADO SEES YOU. (ON THE OTHER HAND, YOU COULD GET YOURSELF A DIFFERENT HOBBY. I'VE HEARD BUNGEE JUMPING OR SNOWBOARDING ARE PRETTY EXCITING BUT RELATIVELY SAFE IN COMPARISON!)

TIP 1

YOU'LL NEED TO GET YOURSELF A REALLY GOOD MAP AND GET TO KNOW THE AREA BEFORE YOU SET OFF. IN FACT, YOU SHOULDN'T REALLY LEAVE HOME WITHOUT A GOOD (HUMAN) GUIDE. I'D TAKE YOU MYSELF, BUT I'M NOT THAT DAFT!

YOU'LL NEED A MOBILE PHONE IN CASE OF EMERGENCIES. AND YOU'LL HAVE TO HAVE SOMEONE ELSE WITH YOU (IF YOU KNOW ANYONE WHO'S NUTTY ENOUGH?) - OR THERE'LL BE NOBODY TO SEND FOR HELP IF YOU RUN INTO TROUBLE!

TIP NUMBER 2...
YOU MIGHT HAVE TO DRIVE 800 KILOMETRES A DAY, SO YOU NEED A COMFORTABLE CAR FOR TRAVELLING. (YOU'LL PROBABLY HAVE TO SLEEP IN IT TOO.) OH, YES, LIGHTNING IS A PRETTY BIG RISK, BUT AT LEAST IF YOU'RE INSIDE YOUR CAR YOU SHOULD BE WELL PROTECTED. (STILL FEEL LIKE GOING?)

TIP 3
AS FOR HIDDEN DANGERS... TO START WITH YOU'LL NEED TO KNOW WHAT YOU'RE LOOKING FOR.
SOME TORNADOES HAVE NICE NEAT FUNNEL SHAPES SO THEY'RE EASY ENOUGH TO IDENTIFY. OTHERS LOOK A REAL MESS. THEY'RE LIKE DIRTY, UNTIDY SWIRLING CLUMPS (PICTURE YOUR HAIR WHEN YOU'VE JUST WOKEN UP!) AND THEY MIGHT BE LURKING BEHIND CLOUDS, HILLS OR TREES. YOU'LL NEED TO KEEP YOUR EYES PEELED AT ALL TIMES.

TIP NUMBER 4...
NOW PROMISE ME YOU WON'T GET TOO CLOSE! TORNADOES ARE TERRIBLY UNPREDICTABLE. IF A TORNADO TURNS NASTY, YOU'LL HAVE TO BE READY TO DROP YOUR CAMERA AND GET OUT OF THE NEIGHBOURHOOD...FAST!

TIP 5

OK, NOW SUPPOSE YOU'VE SPOTTED YOUR TORNADO, BUT IT DOESN'T SEEM TO BE MOVING? DON'T TAKE YOUR EYES OFF IT FOR A SECOND. IT *MIGHT* BE COMING STRAIGHT FOR YOU! DON'T MAKE THE MISTAKE OF TRYING TO DRIVE AWAY FROM IT. IT WILL CATCH YOU UP! INSTEAD DRIVE OFF TO THE SIDE OF THE ROAD... AND WAIT.

WELL, THAT'S ABOUT ALL THE ADVICE I CAN OFFER YOU. NOW TELL ME YOU'RE NOT GOING? YOU'VE CHANGED YOUR MIND? PHEW, THANK GOODNESS FOR THAT, YOU REALLY HAD ME WORRIED!

You might think that weather doesn't get much wilder than this. That tracking tornadoes is as tough as it gets. But you'd be wrong. You're about to meet an even more murderous storm. Hurry along to the next chapter – it'll make your hair stand on end...

HAIR-RAISING HURRICANES

They're hair-raising hurricanes in the Atlantic, thundering typhoons in the Pacific, savage cyclones in the Indian Ocean and in Australia they're known as willy-willies. But call them what you like, they all mean exactly the same thing. Furiously spinning superstorms which rage across tropical seas like gigantic cosmic Catherine wheels. Forget thunderstorms and tornadoes! It's official. HURRICANES ARE THE MOST DANGEROUS STORMS ON EARTH! They claim more lives and cause more damage than all other stormy weather put together.

What on Earth is a hurricane?

A hurricane begins over the sea. But it's a bit choosy about which sea it picks. It must be nice and warm and humid. Somewhere truly tropical, like the Caribbean Sea. The mixture of warmth and water vapour's vital – it's the violent hurricane's ideal lunch, and it's what makes clouds and rain. By the way, a hurricane sucks up about two BILLION tonnes of moisture a day, then chucks it all back down as rain!

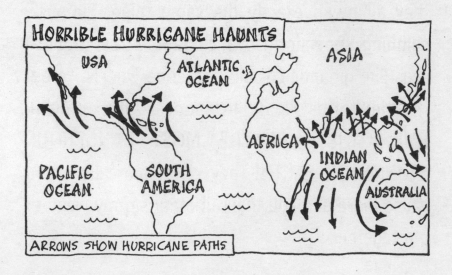

HORRIBLE HURRICANE HAUNTS

USA

ATLANTIC OCEAN

ASIA

PACIFIC OCEAN

SOUTH AMERICA

AFRICA

INDIAN OCEAN

AUSTRALIA

ARROWS SHOW HURRICANE PATHS

Inside a hurricane

1 Warm sea heats air above it. Warm, moist air rises quickly...

2 ...creating low pressure at the surface. More air sweeps in, then starts spiralling upwards.

3 The Earth's rotation (remember the Coriolis force? See page 58) makes the rising air twist round a centre called the eye.

4 Rising air cools, condenses and makes towering thunderclouds and torrential rain.

5 The hurricane spins away. Byeee!

Hurricane winds blow anticlockwise north of the equator and clockwise to the south.

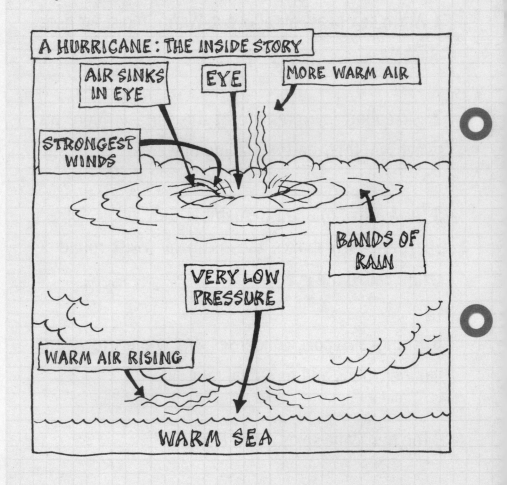

A HURRICANE: THE INSIDE STORY

AIR SINKS IN EYE

EYE

MORE WARM AIR

STRONGEST WINDS

BANDS OF RAIN

VERY LOW PRESSURE

WARM AIR RISING

WARM SEA

Raise the roof with some hair-raising hurricane know-how

ONE THING I CAN SAY FOR CERTAIN ABOUT HURRICANES IS THAT THEY'RE HUGE - HORRIBLY HUGE. I'M TALKING 2,000, YES THAT'S RIGHT, 2,000 TIMES WIDER THAN A TORNADO! THOSE ARE THE REAL BIGGIES OF COURSE, BUT EVEN THE SMALLEST CAN BE ABOUT THE SAME SIZE AS A COUNTRY LIKE ICELAND. THE REAL GIANTS COULD STRETCH FROM ONE SIDE OF AUSTRALIA TO THE OTHER. THEY'RE TALL TOO. UP TO 15 KM HIGH. IMAGINE ALL THAT STORMINESS HANGING OVER YOUR HEAD!

NOW YOU SEE IT!

NOW YOU DON'T!

AUSTRALIA

YOU NEED SOME PRETTY SPEEDY WINDS TO MAKE A HURRICANE, AT LEAST 119 KM AN HOUR TO QUALIFY. OF COURSE BY HURRICANE STANDARDS THAT'S NOTHING, THEY CAN BLOW MUCH HARDER THAN THAT. OH YES, IN A FULL SCALE HURRICANE, THE WINDS ROAR ALONG FASTER THAN AN EXPRESS TRAIN AT OVER 300 KM AN HOUR. YOU'LL FIND THE STRONGEST WINDS IN THE EYE-WALL, THAT'S THE RING OF CLOUDS AROUND THE EYE. THE SMALLER THE EYE, THE FASTER THE WINDS SWIRL. OOOH, JUST THINKING ABOUT IT MAKES ME SHUDDER!

IN THE USA, HURRICANES ARE GRADED ONE TO FIVE, DEPENDING ON WIND SPEED, PRESSURE AND THE DAMAGE THEY DO. GRADE ONE MEANS YOU'VE GOT A PRETTY PATHETIC HURRICANE ON YOUR HANDS, WHICH - LUCKY FOR YOU - WON'T CAUSE TOO MUCH CHAOS. BUT GET UP TO FIVE AND YOU'RE TALKING FULL-SCALE DISASTER. THESE KILLERS ARE GOING TO CAUSE TROUBLE WHEREVER THEY STRIKE. SO MAKE SURE YOU STAY WELL AWAY!

IN THE ATMOSPHERIC ATLANTIC, SOMETHING LIKE 100 STORMS A YEAR LOOK SET TO BECOME FULL-SCALE HAIR-RAISING HURRICANES. BUT YOU CAN RELAX, ONLY SIX OR SEVEN EVER MAKE IT. PHEW! AROUND THE WORLD, ABOUT 35 TROPICAL STORMS A YEAR REACH FULL HURRICANE STATUS. AND THEY HAVE THEIR SEASONS. YOU'D BETTER KEEP AWAY FROM THE ATLANTIC AND NORTHERN PACIFIC OCEANS BETWEEN JUNE AND NOVEMBER. THIS IS WHEN THE SEAS REACH A TOASTY WARM 27°C. SOUTH OF THE EQUATOR AND OFF AUSTRALIA, THE STORM SEASON LASTS FROM NOVEMBER TO MARCH. SO IF YOU'RE THINKING ABOUT IT, APRIL AND MAY LOOK LIKE THE SAFEST MONTHS TO BOOK THAT FOUR-STAR LUXURY OCEAN CRUISE.

FOR SOME WEIRD REASON, SCIENTISTS CALL YOUNG HURRICANES 'SEEDLINGS'. THEY START OUT AS A SMALL CLUSTER OF THUNDERSTORMS, THEN TRAVEL THOUSANDS OF KMS ACROSS THE SEAS BEFORE THEY 'BLOOM' INTO PROPER STORMS. BLOOMING HURRICANES TAKE THEIR TIME TO GET WHERE THEY'RE GOING. BUT THEY CAN KEEP MOVING AT THE SAME PACE, DAY AFTER DAY, NIGHT AFTER NIGHT, FOR A WEEK OR SO, SO THEY CERTAINLY COVER SOME GROUND! I'M KEEPING WELL OUT OF THEIR WAY!

Hurricanes could have their uses. A hurricane is bursting with more energy than 400 nuclear bombs. If you could turn a day's energy from a hurricane into electricity, it would keep the USA in power for six whole months. Which would be absolutely fantastic – think of all the money it would save! There's just one teensy weensy drawback. Nobody knows how to get at this electricity – well, would you fancy trying to collect it up? Thought not.

Eye, eye

In the middle of the swirling wind and cloud is a circular patch of plummeting pressure 45 kilometres wide. The "eye" of the storm. Are you brave enough to look into the eye of a storm? Some gutsy geographers do just that for a living. They fly straight into the eye in special hurricane-hunting aircraft. So why on Earth do they take the risk? Well, it's the only real way to take accurate measurements. This way they can tell how bad the storm is and which way it's heading. (It's also tracked by satellite and radar.) And then they can sound the alarm. Besides, it may be risky but if adventure's what you're after, this is where it's at! As the plucky pilots in this nerve-wracking true story found out.

Eye fliers

At Kessler Air Force Base in Biloxi, Mississippi, Colonel Chuck Coleman had just finished briefing the crew. "A note of caution to end on," he told the small group of men. "The good news is that the Hercules is a very strong

aircraft. We haven't lost one in the two years we've been flying. The bad news is that other groups have lost three since 1947. If you do have to ditch in the ocean, you probably won't need your life jackets — the chance of survival is virtually nil, I'm afraid. Goodbye, men, and good luck."

An hour later, shortly after midnight on 2 September 1977, the crew boarded the huge Hercules WC-130 aircraft standing ready on the runway. They were part of the 920th Weather Reconnaissance Group of the US Air Force, known to everyone as the "Storm Trackers". Their mission was to fly straight into the centre of a full-blown hurricane! Whirling wildly over the Gulf of Mexico, Hurricane Anita had been steadily growing into one of the worst storms in years. A storm that could easily turn into a killer. They had to find out more about her. Already, the National Hurricane Centre in

Miami was busily following Anita's progress. Now the Hercules would fly right into the hurricane's eye to measure and track her path. Once in the eye, the crew would drop a parachute that held a metal cylinder carrying instruments to measure air pressure, temperature and humidity inside the storm. The cylinder was called a dropsonde. A radio transmitter in the dropsonde would transmit data back to the aircraft. At least, that was the plan.

At 1 a.m. the huge plane rumbled down the runway and took off into the pitch black sky. Almost two hours later, dazzling flashes of lightning streaked between sky and the sea far below. Sure signs that they were  nearing the hurricane and their deadly destination.

"Time to strap yourselves in now, guys," the pilot announced. "And make sure that everything else is tied down. We're almost there…"

Just in time. Minutes later, the huge plane began to rock and tip, tossed about by lightning and lashing rain. The navigator's voice crackled over the deafening din. "Looks like the eye's right ahead of us now but the rain's so heavy I can't see anything on the radar. We've got some rough stuff to go through, that's for sure. I'll try and get something on the computer. Damn, we just missed it. Let's go back and have another try."

For more than an hour, the giant plane tried to find a way into the hurricane. But each time, howling winds and driving rain blocked its path. It was as if the storm itself was trying to keep them out. At almost four in the morning, the navigator's voice was heard again. "Wait a minute," he said. "We've got something up ahead. And it looks very much like a hole!"

"Everybody tied down back there?" queried the pilot. "It's going to be a bumpy ride."

"Roger, everything's snug as a bug in a rug," came the reply.

The pilot was right. Suddenly the heavy plane

lurched up and down, as if it was about to break apart. Anxious moments followed as the pilot expertly guided the plane right into the hurricane. Now they were flying through the hurricane's eye wall, where the strongest, fiercest winds were felt. The plane was thrashing about now, tossed to and fro by the awesome air currents as if it was light as a feather. The rain was a solid mass of water falling from masses of heaving black clouds. It was terrifying.

For several nail-biting minutes, the crew held their breath. Then, suddenly, the horror stopped. "We've got it," announced the relieved pilot. "We're in the eye now. And it looks like it's about 22 kilometres across." They had made it.

Once inside the eye, the crew set to work fixing the storm's location and sending data from the dropsonde back to the Hurricane Centre in Miami. They had only 45 minutes to complete their task. Then they turned back, out of the eye, and through the raging wind and rain. If the outward journey had been terrible, the return journey was even worse. But finally, at 9 a.m., the plane limped back to base, shaken but safe, and touched down again at Kessler.

Luckily, Hurricane Anita wasn't a killer. The Storm Trackers had done a good job. Their findings meant that hurricane warnings were issued early, people living in the path of the storm as it surged inland were evacuated to safety, and the crew had a trip they would never forget.

But why did things suddenly change when they reached the centre of the hurricane. What sort of weather did they find in the eye? Was it...

a) wild and windy

b) freezing and foggy

c) calm and clear?

ANSWER

Answer: **c)** Amazingly, the weather in the eye of a hurricane is wonderful, with clear blue skies and light winds. Completely unlike the chaos raging all around. In fact, it's so clear here you can sometimes see the surface of the sea below and the stars above. Sometimes pilots have seen thousands of spooked-out seabirds trapped in this circle of calm. If you're on land, there's a break in the storm as the eye passes overhead. Don't be fooled, though – what you should do now is take cover! It's only the calm before the other half of the storm comes blasting past.

171

Name that hurricane

As soon as a hurricane is spotted, it's given a name to avoid any mix-ups later on. The names are taken from a list, drawn up in alphabetical order. A new one's made up each year.

Naming hurricanes started in 1890 with Australian weatherman Clement L. Wragge. He was called 'Wet' Wragge by his enemies, and he certainly had plenty of those. He was always falling out with people, particularly stuck-up politicians. They were so stubborn and unreasonable. He wrote them letter after letter filled with helpful hints about running the country, but did they take any notice? Did they heck.

"Dear Mr Wragge," went their replies. "Thank you for your most interesting letters. Unfortunately, we're far too busy to read them all now. Sorry."

Grrr! Clement was furious. He decided to get his own back.

But how? What was the most vicious thing he could think of? Something even a politician wouldn't want to be associated with. He had it! What else but the meanest, moodiest, stormiest weather he could think of – a horrible hurricane, of course. So he began naming hurricanes after particularly pesky politicians. Who were not best pleased.

The twentieth century system of naming storms began with a music-loving American radio operator.

It was during the time of the Second World War. As his colleague broadcast news of a storm to a US aircraft pilot, he could be heard in the background … whistling! The song on his lips was the catchily titled "Every little breeze seems to whisper Louise". The storm was immediately named Louise and the custom stuck. After this, hurricanes were named after women, usually weathermen's wives or girlfriends. Until they complained and men's names were added to the list. Especially horrible hurricanes have their names taken off the list so they are never used again. There'll never be another Hurricane Andrew, or Carol, or Flora, or Klaus. Can you think of anyone you'd like to name a hurricane after? What about your favourite geography teacher?

WATCH OUT, HERE COMES HURRICANE HEALY!

ARE YOU TALKING A LOAD OF HOT-AIR AGAIN, TOMKINS?

But names can be horribly misleading. Some of these hurricanes might sound as if they wouldn't hurt a fly then they go and cause dreadful chaos and destruction. One of the worst ever hurricanes to hit the USA didn't sound in the least like a monster. In fact it sounded rather sweet. Hah! Prepare to meet monstrous Hurricane Camille.

Pass Christian, Mississippi, USA, August 1969

Early on 17 August 1969, most people living along the Mississippi coast were busy boarding up their homes and businesses and heading inland – fast. The area was on full-scale hurricane alert – Hurricane Camille, labelled by the experts an "extremely dangerous storm", was on its way. As the day wore on, the roads leading inland became clogged with traffic, as the threat from the hurricane grew. Radio and television stations carried minute-by-minute warnings while the police and the town's officials urged people to evacuate.

But some people ignored their pleas to leave town. They'd made other plans for the evening.

You are invited to a

HURRICANE PARTY

at the
Richelieu Apartments,
Pass Christian,
Mississippi

On 17 August 1969 from 8 till late

Please bring a bottle to
set things spinning

R.S.V.P.

Instead of getting out of town, residents of these luxury beachfront apartments in Pass Christian decided to throw a "hurricane-watch" party and sit out the storm. They'd stocked up with food and drink and invited their friends round for a good time. They expected to watch the storm from a distance, thinking it would strike many kilometres to the east. But it didn't. At the last minute, Camille veered westwards and smashed ashore at ... Pass Christian. It was 10.30 p.m. The hurricane party was in full swing. So was the party-pooping hurricane.

What the party-goers didn't know was that the Richelieu Apartments lay directly in the path of the worst winds and of the massive waves stirred up by the storm. These crashed ashore with devastating results. Afterwards, nothing was left of the apartment building but its concrete base. Worse still, only one of the 24 guests invited to the party survived. Later she told her story.

Mrs Mary Anne Gerlach was getting ready to go to the party with husband Fritz when the storm struck. The Gerlachs had attended hurricane parties before and were looking forward to this one. They never made it. By now, massive waves were hammering against the window of their second-floor living room.

Mrs Gerlach described what happened next, "We went into our bedroom and in a few minutes heard an awful popping sound as the windows smashed. We held our shoulders to the door to try to keep the water out. But in about five minutes, the bed was floating halfway to the ceiling. And you could feel the building swaying like a boat. I just knew then that I was going to die."

Somehow, Mrs Gerlach managed to swim out of a window, clutching a pillow as a float.

Outside, she was swept into a treetop almost eight kilometres from the beach, and there she stayed until morning. Or so she said...

Since then, another survivor, Ben Duckworth, has claimed that the infamous hurricane party never happened. He says the residents were too tired from boarding up windows to dance the night away. What's certainly true is that Hurricane Camille was a killer. It was officially classified as a Category 5 hurricane, one of only two to strike the USA in the 20th century. A total of 258 people were killed; 68 declared missing and damage was estimated at £1 billion.

Serious side-effects

But it's not just the storms themselves that do the damage – they can have serious side effects. Nine out of ten people who die in hurricanes are killed by storm surges. Take Hurricane Katrina, for starters. In August 2005, Katrina crashed into the Gulf Coast of the USA, with catastrophic results. The hurricane triggered a massive storm surge nine metres high. Here's what happens. The sea beneath the hurricane bulges. Then the wind blasts the bulge along, until it crashes on to the coast. Katrina's storm surge smashed through New Orleans' flood defences, flooding 80 per cent of the city, and killing and injuring thousands of people. The clean-up continues today.

Stormiest weather ever

However closely you keep track of a hurricane, you can never be certain what it'll do next. Horrible hurricanes are full of surprises, changing course when you least expect it. As the people of Darwin, Australia, found out. On Christmas Day 1974, Cyclone Tracy smashed the city to pieces and killed

66 people. It was meant to pass safely by many miles offshore.

So, is there anything at all that meteorologists can do to hunt down hurricanes and stop them in their tracks? The answer is yes — at least they're trying. With modern bits and bobs, like aircraft, satellites and supercomputers, stormy forecasting is getting better all the time. And the earlier warnings can be given, the more lives can be saved. But staying one step ahead of a storm isn't easy.

SERIOUS STORM-WATCHING

Scientists who study stormy weather are called meteorologists (meet-ee-or-ol-ogists). But what on Earth does meteorology have to do with the weather? Actually, it comes from an Ancient Greek word which meant the study of, well, anything above the ground. Pretty vague, eh? Especially as this included astronomy, and the study of meteors – which are lumps of rock which break off comets and whizz through space. And have nothing to do with the weather! To clear things up, the Greeks later split astronomy and meteorology up and made meteorology the study of the weather – only we now know that meteors have NOTHING to do with the weather! But the name stuck all the same!

Meteorology moves on

One of the first serious meteorologists was Aristotle. He was Greek and lived in the 4th century BCE. In about 340 BCE, he wrote the first ever weather book. It was called the *Meteorologica* (meet-ee-or-ol-ogica). What a mouthful! In it, Aristotle set out his new ideas. Even though he didn't get everything right, people believed his ideas for almost two thousand years.

In the sixteenth century, things took a seriously scientific turn. Horrible geographers started to do real weather experiments instead of just staring at the stormy skies. They also invented new instruments for measuring and recording what the weather did. Remember Torricelli? This is when he invented the barometer, and when his very own geography teacher, Galileo Galilei, invented the thermoscope (an earlier version of the thermometer).

Earth-shattering fact

Until half way through the nineteenth century, people often didn't know that a storm was brewing until it blew up in their faces. There were no phones, and the post was hopeless! Then in 1844 American Samuel Morse hit on a brilliant new way of sending messages, using his new-fangled invention, the electric telegraph.

BOOM!

COULD BE WE'RE IN FOR A SPELL OF BAD WEATHER

By the end of the century, telegraph lines linked many big cities. They even ran between Europe and America. So what's all this got to do with the weather? It meant that vital information could be sent long distances, and fast. I mean what was the point of knowing a storm was brewing in Britain if you lived in America and couldn't tell anyone about it?

Could you be a meteorologist?

Nowadays there are thousands of meteorologists all over the world trying to suss out stormy weather. The more they find out, the more lives and homes can be saved. The good news is that they're learning all the time. The bad news is that meteorology is not an exact science. Which means things can go wrong. Horribly wrong. You can blame the awkward atmosphere for this. The way it changes by the second makes it extremely tricky to track.

Have you got what it takes to be a meteorologist? Is watching stormy weather the job for you? Before you start the first lesson, answer these three simple questions.

1 Are you a maths megabrain? Yes/No
2 A whizz with computers? Yes/No
3 Have you got good eyesight? Yes/No

How did you do?

If you answered yes to all three questions, congratulations! Go straight to step one. A lot of meteorology means doing long sums and working things out on computers. So if you find maths murder, you might be stumped. (You could always become a geography teacher instead. Ask yours what she's like at maths!) Good eyesight's useful because, even with heaps of horribly high-tech equipment, the best way to keep an eye on the weather is to stand outside and look!

Six easy steps to making it in meteorology

Here's mega-brain Mona to explain how it's done:

STEP 1: GET THE MEASURE OF THE WEATHER

YOU'VE GOT TO START BY GETTING A GOOD PICTURE OF WHAT THE WEATHER'S UP TO. THIS MEANS MEASURING THINGS LIKE WIND, AIR PRESSURE AND RAINFALL.

AND FOR THIS, YOU'LL WANT YOUR OWN WEATHER STATION. THIS IS THE SORT OF EQUIPMENT YOU'D BE LIKELY TO NEED. SOME OF IT'S A BIT EXPENSIVE, SO YOU COULD HAVE A GO AT MAKING SOME BASIC BITS YOURSELF.

A BAROMETER FOR MEASURING AIR PRESSURE. UNITS USED ARE MILLIBARS. SEE THE CHAPTER ON AWESOME ATMOSPHERE FOR MORE INFO ABOUT THE AIR.

A THERMOMETER FOR MEASURING TEMPERATURE. UNITS USED ARE DEGREES CELSIUS (°C) OR DEGREES FAHRENHEIT (°F). (SEE OPPOSITE TO FIND OUT MORE.)

METEOROLOGISTS KEEP THEIR INSTRUMENTS IN A WOODEN BOX CALLED A STEPHENSON SCREEN TO PROTECT THEM FROM THE SUN AND WIND.

A CUP ANEMOMETER FOR MEASURING WIND SPEED. UNITS USED ARE KM/H.

CHECK OUT MY NOTES ON HOW TO MAKE YOUR OWN ON THE NEXT PAGE...

The temperature scales were named after two budding scientists, Gabriel Fahrenheit (1686–1736) and Anders Celsius (1701–1744). Young Gabriel had a good start in life. He was born in Poland in 1686 and his family had pots of money. But things soon went horribly wrong. When he was just 15, both his parents died after devouring some dodgy mushrooms. Poor orphan Gabriel ran away to seek his fame and fortune in Europe. Lucky for him, he found friends in high places. One of them was a Danish scientist, Olaf Romer. Old Olaf's great passion was thermometers and he encouraged Gabriel to make his own. But brainy Gabriel went one better and added his very own temperature scale. It began at 32°F, the melting point of ice and went up to 212°F, the boiling point of water. Seems an odd place to start and finish, but it quickly caught on and is still used in some countries. Did it bring Gabriel fame or fortune? No way. He died without a penny to his name.

Anders Celsius was quite another kettle of, er, fish. For a start, he was a posh professor and taught astronomy at a top Swedish university. He devised another scale which started at 0°C and went up to 100°C. Which made it a whole lot easier to remember.

CONJURE UP YOUR OWN ANEMOMETER

WHAT YOU NEED:

- FOUR YOGHURT POTS (eat the yoghurt and wash pots first)
- TWO STICKS OF BALSA WOOD, ABOUT 30 CM LONG
- THREE LARGE BEADS
- ONE NAIL (and a handy grown up to bash it in for you!)
- GLUE
- ONE WOODEN POST

WHAT TO DO:

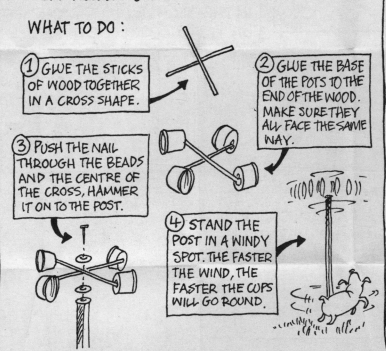

1. GLUE THE STICKS OF WOOD TOGETHER IN A CROSS SHAPE.

2. GLUE THE BASE OF THE POTS TO THE END OF THE WOOD. MAKE SURE THEY ALL FACE THE SAME WAY.

3. PUSH THE NAIL THROUGH THE BEADS AND THE CENTRE OF THE CROSS, HAMMER IT ON TO THE POST.

4. STAND THE POST IN A WINDY SPOT. THE FASTER THE WIND, THE FASTER THE CUPS WILL GO ROUND.

A WIND SOCK OR WIND VANE FOR MEASURING WIND DIRECTION. UNITS USED ARE THE FOUR POINTS OF THE COMPASS (N, S, E, W) AND THE FOUR POINTS IN BETWEEN (NE, SE, NW, SW).

TO MAKE YOUR OWN WIND VANE YOU COULD STICK A SOCK ON THE END OF A STICK, BUT YOU DON'T NEED TO BOTHER — ANOTHER WAY OF TELLING WHICH WAY THE WIND'S BLOWING IS TO LICK YOUR FINGER AND STICK IT IN THE AIR, TURN IT UNTIL THE WET BIT FEELS COOL IN THE WIND.

✓

WIND SOCK

✗ PHWOAR!

SMELLY SOCK

RAIN GOES IN HERE

A RAIN GAUGE FOR MEASURING RAIN FALL. UNITS USED ARE MILLIMETRES. THIS CAN ALSO BE USED TO MEASURE SNOW.

MILLIMETRES

194

A HYGROMETER FOR MEASURING HUMIDITY. UNITS USED ARE DEGREES CELSIUS(°C) DEGREES FAHRENHEIT(°F).

ONE KIND IS CALLED A PSYCHROMETER (OR A WET AND DRY BULB THERMOMETER). IT'S LIKE A DOUBLE THERMOMETER. THE "DRY BULB" MEASURES TEMPERATURE. THE "WET BULB" HAS ONE END WRAPPED IN DAMP CLOTH SO IT CAN DETECT WATER VAPOUR IN THE AIR. THE HUMIDITY IS THE DIFFERENCE BETWEEN THE TWO READINGS. SIMPLE!

OKTAS

CLEAR SKY

1 OKTA OF COVER

2 OKTAS OF COVER

3 OKTAS OF COVER

4 OKTAS OF COVER

5 OKTAS OF COVER

6 OKTAS OF COVER

7 OKTAS OF COVER

8 OKTAS OF COVER

SKY OBSCURED; FOG

YOU DON'T NEED ANY FANCY EQUIPMENT TO CALCULATE CLOUD COVER - THIS IS WHERE YOUR EAGLE EYE-SIGHT COMES IN. FIRST, STAND WHERE YOU CAN GET A GOOD VIEW OF THE SKY. DIVIDE THE SKY IN HALF, THEN IN HALF AGAIN. (OK, SO YOU'LL HAVE TO USE YOUR IMAGINATION!) HOW MUCH OF IT IS COVERED BY CLOUD? ONE SECTION? TWO? ONE AND A HALF? TIMES THIS BY TWO. THIS GIVES YOU THE ANSWER IN EIGHTHS, OR OKTAS, AS THEY'RE TECHNICALLY KNOWN. GOOD TERM FOR IMPRESSING YOUR TEACHER, EH? OKTAS ARE UNITS USED TO MEASURE CLOUD.

HOW TO PREDICT A STORM

What you do:

Check your instruments and write down the results in your notebook. Every day, twice a day, morning and evening. Even at the weekend (so no more lounging about in bed), 365 days a year. After all, that's what I have to do, EVERY day!

But at least you won't be alone. There are about 11,000 weather stations around the world busily collecting data. Some are run by professional meteorologists, like me. Others rely on helpers, like you. And then there are the high-tech weather ships, planes and satellites.

What to do with your results:

So how can you tell if a storm's brewing from your results? Here's how.

Have you found out any of these things happening?

- Pressure falling?
- Rain getting heavier?
- Clouds gathering?
- Humidity rising?
- Winds getting stronger?

Do your results show all of these happening at the same time? Congratulations, you've predicted a thunderstorm. Quick, get inside, get comfy, and watch from a safe distance.

STEP 2: SNEAK A SNAP FROM A SATELLITE

OK, THIS IS WHERE THE EQUIPMENT STARTS GETTING SERIOUSLY EXPENSIVE. IT'S UNLIKELY YOU COULD AFFORD A WEATHER SATELLITE - WELL, I CERTAINLY COULDN'T. WEATHER SATELLITES HAVE TO BE POSITIONED THOUSANDS OF KILOMETRES UP IN THE SKY TO KEEP A CONSTANT EYE ON OUR STORMY PLANET. (JUST GETTING IT UP THERE IS GOING TO COST A LARGE FORTUNE.) THEY'RE THE SAME SORT OF SATELLITES THAT BRING YOU SATELLITE TV, BUT THEY HAVE GOT ON-BOARD CAMERAS THAT SNAP PICTURES OF CLOUDS AND STORMS AND BEAM THEM BACK TO EARTH. THEY CAN SHOW ALL SORTS OF THINGS, LIKE A HURRICANE COMING!

STEP 3: RAID A RADAR READ-OUT

ONCE A SATELLITE'S SPOTTED A STORM, RADAR CAN TAKE OVER TO TRACK IT. HEAVY RAIN FROM STORMS UP TO 320 KILOMETRES AWAY SHOWS UP WHITE ON A SCREEN. ORDINARY RADAR SHOWS YOU THE RAIN'S THERE. AND THE NEW HIGH-TECH DOPPLER RADAR SHOWS YOU WHICH WAY IT'S HEADING. VERY USEFUL.

WHICH IS WHY THE US NATIONAL WEATHER SERVICE HAS A STRING OF RADARS ALONG THE COAST FOR TRACKING DOWN HURRICANES AND TORNADOES. SOUNDS INTERESTING? DON'T MISS THIS WEEK'S SPECIAL OFFER- IF YOU THINK YOU CAN AFFORD IT!

STEP 4: PLUG IN YOUR COMPUTER

ONCE YOU'VE GOT THE DATA, WHAT ON EARTH DO YOU DO WITH IT? THIS IS WHERE A COMPUTER GENIUS COMES IN HANDY. EVERYTHING HAS TO BE TURNED INTO NUMBERS AND FED INTO YOUR SUPER-COMPUTER, MORE EXPENSE I'M AFRAID. MORE ON COMPUTERS OVER THE PAGE...

OVER THE LAST DECADES, SUPERCOMPUTERS HAVE REVOLUTIONIZED WEATHER FORECASTING. THE WORLD METEOROLOGICAL ORGANIZATION (WMO, FOR SHORT) HAS THREE NUMBER-CRUNCHING CENTRES, IN WASHINGTON DC, USA, MELBOURNE, AUSTRALIA AND MOSCOW, RUSSIA. IN BRITAIN, THE COMPUTER AT THE MET OFFICE IN EXETER CAN PROCESS 16,000 TRILLION CALCULATIONS EVERY SECOND. AROUND 10 MILLION WEATHER OBSERVATIONS A DAY ARE USED TO MAKE THE FORECASTS YOU SEE AND HEAR.

Earth-shattering fact

The first person to bring maths into meteorology was British scientist, Lewis Fry Richardson (1881–1953). Mind you, he didn't have a supercomputer to help him. By hand, it took him three whole months to work out the weather 24 hours ahead! Er ... seems like there was a bit of a flaw in his system. Instead of the supercomputer, he had to make do with several pads of paper and a couple of pens! To do the sums fast enough, he'd have needed 64,000 helpers working flat out! Imagine his relief when electronic computers were invented in 1945.

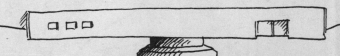

STEP 5: DASH OFF A WEATHER MAP

DON'T PANIC - YOU DON'T HAVE TO BE ANY GOOD AT ART. LET YOUR COMPUTER TAKE THE STRAIN. IT'LL PLOT THE DATA YOU'VE GIVEN IT ON TO A WEATHER MAP. AND UPDATE IT EVERY HOUR. CLEVER. IT CAN DRAW REALLY DETAILED MAPS WHICH COVER THE WHOLE PLANET BY DIVIDING THE SURFACE INTO SQUARES LIKE A GRID. THE MAPS YOU SEE ON THE TELLY AND IN THE NEWSPAPERS ARE MUCH, MUCH SIMPLER VERSIONS OF THESE.

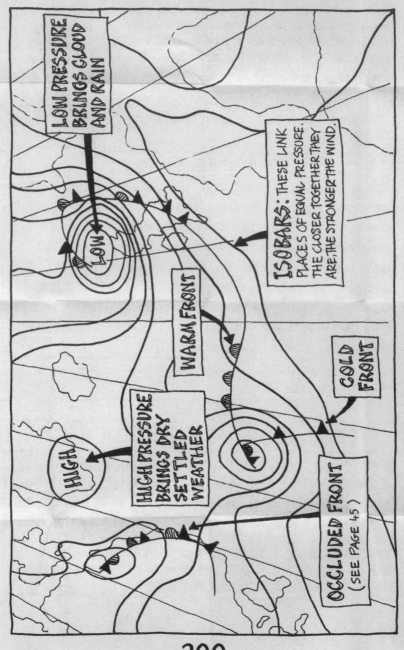

LOW PRESSURE BRINGS CLOUD AND RAIN

ISOBARS: THESE LINK PLACES OF EQUAL PRESSURE. THE CLOSER TOGETHER THEY ARE, THE STRONGER THE WIND.

LOW

WARM FRONT

COLD FRONT

HIGH

HIGH PRESSURE BRINGS DRY SETTLED WEATHER

OCCLUDED FRONT (SEE PAGE 45)

METEOROLOGISTS USE WEATHER MAPS TO PLOT THE WEATHER AND TO WORK OUT WHAT IT'S GOING TO DO. YOUR COMPUTER WILL COME UP WITH A FORECAST, WHICH IS HANDY, BUT THEN IT'S DOWN TO YOU. YOU NEED TO CHECK THAT IT'S GOT IT RIGHT! TRICKY. AND THE ONLY WAY TO TELL IF YOUR FORECAST'S ACCURATE IS TO WAIT A FEW DAYS AND SEE. BY WHICH TIME, IT'LL BE TOO LATE TO CHANGE IT. BUT AT LEAST YOU CAN SEE IF YOU'RE DOING IT RIGHT. MOST METEOROLOGISTS ARE GETTING BETTER ALL THE TIME. SHORT-RANGE FORECASTS (FOR UP TO THREE DAYS AHEAD) ARE NOW ABOUT 86 PER CENT ACCURATE. THIS MEANS THEY'RE RIGHT ABOUT SIX TIMES OUT OF SEVEN. NOT BAD EH? LONG-RANGE FORECASTS ARE MUCH LESS RELIABLE. IF YOUR FORECAST WASN'T UP TO SCRATCH, DON'T WORRY, EVEN THE EXPERTS SOMETIMES GET THINGS WRONG. BADLY WRONG!

Southern England, 16 October 1987

On the night of 15 October 1987, Britain was devastated by its worst storm for almost three hundred years. Most unusual for a country where the weather's normally quite mild – quite mild winters, quite mild summers, quite mild winds, you get the picture? For four terrifying hours, the south of the country felt the storm's full fury, battered by winds howling at over 185 kilometres per hour. Incredibly, only 18 people died. This was because the storm struck at night when most people were in bed and there was very little traffic on the roads. If it had arrived a few hours earlier, when people were still out and about, the death toll would probably have been much higher.

But when people woke up on 16 October, few could believe their eyes. The storm caused an awesome amount of damage – the bill came to a total of about £1.5 billion. Some 19 million trees had been uprooted – many had fallen on cars or houses. One in six homes in the south suffered some damage. Some had their windows blown in; others had their roofs blown off. Seven million people had no electricity while 150,000 phone lines went dead. Hundreds of shops and schools stayed closed. And because roads and railways into London were blocked, the city very nearly came to a complete standstill.

Unfortunately, almost right up to the last minute, meteorologists had no idea what lay in store. When a worried woman rang up the Met Office to see how bad the storm would be, the forecasters even went on TV and said there would be no hurricane. That sort of thing didn't happen in Britain.

So how did they get things so horribly wrong?

Five gale-force facts about the Great Storm

1 People often call the storm of 1987 a hurricane. But they're wrong. True, the winds gusted at hurricane force – more than 119 kilometres per hour – but a hurricane is a tropical storm, and Britain is far too chilly for that. Officially, it ranked as a severe storm. Which was hair-raising enough.

2 But a hurricane had a hand in things. The storm began in the Bay of Biscay, off the Atlantic coast of France and Spain. So far, so normal. Weird things began to happen when it got an unexpected boost. Very warm air connected with Hurricane Floyd (which had been battering the coast of Florida, USA) crossed the Atlantic…

3 …and linked up with the storm. This created what American meteorologists call a bomb. But what would it do next? Bombs are horribly hard to predict. Some fizzle quietly away. Others go off with a bang. Which is exactly what this one did. The storm joined forces and headed towards England.

4 Meteorologists saw a storm brewing over the Atlantic several days earlier. Ships in the Bay of Biscay were advised to get out of the way. But most of the Met Office's weather observations come from ships. If there weren't any left in the Atlantic, they couldn't sound the alarm about the coming storm.

5 Just over two years later, on 25 January 1990, another superstorm struck Britain. This time 47 lives were lost. Meteorologists were better prepared but they still couldn't precisely predict the storm's path. But things are already looking up. Storms which hit southern England early in 1998 were accurately predicted.

Wise up to the weather

So, what if there's a hitch with your high-tech equipment? What if your computer loses the plot? Time to try some old-fashioned weather folklore.

BEST WEATHER PET COMPETITION

THINKING OF GETTING A NEW PET?
FORGET CATS AND DOGS! YOU WANT A
PET YOU CAN REALLY RELY ON, AT LEAST
WHERE FORECASTING THE WEATHER IS CONCERNED.
A PET THAT WILL TELL YOU WHEN IT WANTS TO GO FOR A WALK

2 COWS ARE VERY SENSITIVE TO DAMP, STORMY WEATHER. THEY LIE DOWN OR HUDDLE IN A CORNER OF THEIR FIELD. PERHAPS THEY DON'T LIKE THE FEEL OF SOGGY GRASS SO THEY FIND A NICE, DRY PLACE TO SNUGGLE DOWN ON BEFORE IT STARTS TO RAIN?

1 CONGRATULATIONS! SWALLOWS AND SWIFTS! WHEN THESE WEATHER WISE BIRDS SOAR HIGH IN THE SKY, TAKE COVER. A THUNDERSTORM IS ON ITS WAY. THIS IS BECAUSE THE INSECTS THEY FEED ON GET BLOWN UPWARDS BY RISING AIR CURRENTS THAT OFTEN HAPPEN BEFORE THUNDERSTORMS.

3 WHEN SQUIRRELS START COLLECTING NUTS, WINTER'S ROUND THE CORNER. IGNORE THE SCIENTISTS! THEY'LL TELL YOU THAT SQUIRRELS DO THIS IN AUTUMN ANYWAY. WINTER COULD BE WEEKS OFF. SPOILSPORTS!

The more accurate weather forecasts can be, the better for everyone. Even if you're only picking a good day to have your friends round for a game of open-air tiddlywinks. They'll never be foolproof, but with all the high-tech equipment meteorologists now have to play with, they're getting better all the time. For people living in the path of storms, they can make a huge difference. Really huge — the difference between life and death.

WEATHERING THE STORM

As you're slumped in a comfy armchair, reading this book, meteorologists everywhere are hard at work trying to solve the mysteries of stormy weather. But no matter how expert their forecasting skills, they can't always tell where a storm will strike next. Or when. The terrible truth is that storms sometimes whirl in without warning. And it's not just lives that are lost. Storms can wreck people's homes and businesses and devastate a farmer's entire crop and livelihood, not to mention your dad's prize begonias. So just how horribly hazardous can they be?

Killer storms

Living on an island in the middle of the sunny Caribbean Sea sounds perfect, doesn't it? But nothing is ever quite as it seems. The people of the Caribbean islands know only too well how horribly hazardous stormy weather can be. In 1988, ghastly Hurricane Gilbert took just ten days to turn their lives upside down.

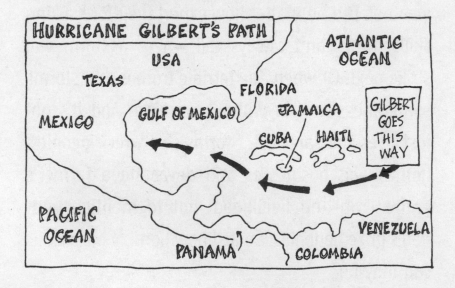

Ghastly Gilbert facts:

1 One of the fiercest storms in history, Gilbert was rated a Category 5 hurricane, also known as a 'supercane'. And you don't get bigger than that.

2 It had the strongest winds ever recorded in a hurricane – with gusts blowing up to a howling 289.9 kilometres per hour.

3 In the eye, the pressure plummeted to 888 millibars, the lowest ever recorded in the western hemisphere until Hurricane Wilma in 2005.

4 Despite its monstrous size, Gilbert had one of the smallest 'eyes' of any hurricane at only 13 kilometres wide (they're usually around 45 kilometres). This concentrated the storm's energy and made it doubly deadly... which was doubly bad news for the people living in the hurricane's path.

So how on Earth did people cope?

1 Jamaica suffered most from the storm. Homes, schools and hospitals were all hit hard. The roof blew off the main telephone exchange and rain poured in all over the equipment – so it's not surprising that they lost all phone links to other countries. For days after the storm they had no electricity, no radio, no television, and no way of telling what on Earth was going on.

2 The Prime Minister of Jamaica said that the storm was "the worst disaster in the modern history of Jamaica". And it was true! For Jamaicans, bananas and chickens were a main source of income. But with battered banana crops and chickens dead, both industries were ruined. Jamaica lost a whole year's worth of earnings!

3 Americans living along the Gulf Coast had just

two days' notice to get ready for the worst. The best thing to do was to get away fast, but people who stayed behind quickly got busy buying emergency food rations and boarding up doors and windows with plywood. Some painted messages on them:

But Gilbert didn't want to know!

4 Thousands of oil workers had to leave their oil rigs in the Gulf of Mexico. They were right in the path of the storm. Only a week before, another hurricane, called Florence, had sent them fleeing for the shore.

Two hurricanes in two weeks – how unlucky can you get?

5 In the town of Corpus Christi, Texas, poor old Gilbert Gonzales was pestered with phone calls from his (so-called) friends. For some strange reason they blamed him for Hurricane Gilbert's nasty nature! Meanwhile, local radio stations played suitably stormy songs, such as "Blowin' in the Wind", "Riders on the Storm" and, of course, "Stormy Weather", to try to cheer people up!

Earth-shattering fact

Incredibly, while most people were trying their best to escape, some scientists were flying hundreds of tracker aircraft straight into the hurricane's 'eye'. In fact, there were so many planes that collisions became a serious risk and emergency action had to be taken to co-ordinate their flight paths.

Storm survival

So what can you do if a hurricane looks likely? Well, the most important thing is to sound the alarm, and fast. But meteorologists have to get the timing just right. If they warn people too soon before they are certain about the path of the hurricane, they might start to panic for no reason. If the alarm is given too late, there won't be time to get everyone out. Very tricky. In the USA, the alert is given in two stages. First, they issue a hurricane 'watch' 48 hours before they think a hurricane might strike, and they make sure the emergency services are ready for action. Then, a hurricane 'warning' is issued 36 hours ahead when experts have a better idea where the storm will hit.

STORMY WEATHER WARNING ☠

THE PROBLEM IS THAT HURRICANES ARE HORRIBLY UNPREDICTABLE - RIGHT UP TO THE LAST MOMENT. SO EVEN THE 24-HOUR WARNING CAN STILL GET THE PATH WRONG BY AS MUCH AS 80 KM. AND THE WAIT CAN BE TERRIFYING.

Earth-shattering fact

A place that learnt storm safety the hard way was the holiday resort of Galveston, Texas. The town was built on a low-lying sand spit. BIG mistake. When a lethal hurricane hit in 1900, it stirred up a massive storm surge. By evening, the town lay under four metres of water; 6-8,000 people were dead and 2,700 homes had been swept away. Galveston was rebuilt, with a secret weapon — a brand-new barrier to keep the sea out. And it worked! When another storm struck 15 years later, fewer than 300 people died.

STORMY WEATHER SAFETY MANUAL

So if there's a hurricane or tornado coming to a place near you, here's what you should do. Right, now pay attention - one day it could be YOU!

① You'll need to keep a close ear to the radio - it'll broadcast urgent warnings and tell you what to do. There'll be news on the TV too but you might not be able to watch it because the storm will probably have blown the power lines down.

② Get out of the way! Leave town if you can. But whatever happens, head inland away from the coast. This is no time for a holiday and besides, the hurricane will come in from the sea!

③ If you're stuck in town, try getting to an emergency shelter. These are usually set up in public places like churches and schools. But if you're not sure where to go, try to think of somewhere that's underground. Remember Tornado Alley? There, most homes have a tornado shelter in the cellar. If you don't have one you could always try making your own! (TURN TO THE NEXT PAGE.)

DO YOU HAVE FIRE DRILLS AT SCHOOL? WHY NOT HAVE A HURRICANE DRILL INSTEAD? TO BE ON THE SAFE SIDE, PLACES USED TO STORMY WEATHER HOLD PRACTICE DRILLS SO THEY'RE READY FOR THE REAL THING. WISE MOVE!

Sink your own storm shelter

What you need:

- two pieces of heavy wood
- lots of concrete (or a concrete cylinder)
- a spade

What you do:

a) Dig a big hole under your house about 1.5 metres wide, 2.5 metres long and 2 metres deep. This is big enough to hold eight people. (It might be best to check with your parents before you start.)

b) Line it with concrete or bury the cylinder in it. (If time's running out, forget the concrete. Get into the hole ... fast.)

c) Make some doors out of the wood.

d) Stock the shelter with food and water.

e) Get inside and hold on … tight!

4 You haven't got a storm shelter? It's OK, no need to panic. If you've got time, you can always board up your windows and doors and move any furniture away from the windows. You can buy permanent storm shutters, or use sheets of plywood. Now, move to a room in the middle of the house. If it's the bathroom, get into the bath for extra safety. Whatever you do, stay away from windows or mirrors – flying glass can be deadly. And, please, please, PLEASE – DON'T go outside for a peek.

5 Wherever you get to, stay put until the storm is well and truly over – particularly if it's a hurricane.

And don't let the storm fool you. If the weather suddenly turns calm and peaceful stay right where you are. This could just be the eye of the storm, remember, with the rest of the storm right behind!

6 Keep your survival kit packed and ready. You'll need drinking water (to be on the safe side – take enough for a few days), tinned food (but don't forget the tin-opener), sleeping bags, a first-aid kit, a torch (with plenty of batteries). Make sure your radio works on batteries too.

BRING ON THE STORM, I'M READY!

THE STORM PASSED WHILE YOU WERE GETTING READY!

7 But what if you're caught outside? Stay calm. Find a ditch and lie down flat, or shelter under a sturdy bridge.

Keep your head covered, in case of any flying debris. Whatever you do, DON'T wait out a hurricane or tornado in your car — it'll be useless against the howling winds. Get out and lie flat or get into a shelter … fast.

Earth-shattering fact

Got good hearing? Keeping your ear to the ground is the latest way of telling if a tornado is coming. Honestly! As a tornado hops across land, it sends shock waves shooting through the ground. If you listen hard, you can hear them. But the good news is that you soon won't have to put your own ears at risk. Scientists in the USA are busy working on an electronic ear which will do the job for you. The idea is to fit one in your home, a bit like having a burglar alarm.

Every cloud has a silver lining

In the past, people tried all sorts of ways of scaring off storms from ringing bells at them to shooting them with cannon. But is it possible to tame a tornado? Could you really halt a hurricane's power? Some American scientists tried to find out.

In the 1940s, scientists discovered a new way to make rain. They made a dust from a chemical called silver iodide and sprinkled it by aircraft into some storm clouds. This dust made ice crystals grow in the clouds. The ice crystals then melted and fell as rain. So far, so good. Until they tried to do the same with a hurricane. They wanted to drop some silver iodide into the eye wall so the hurricane would make lots of rain. The rain would use up lots of energy that would make the eye wall bigger and the winds weaker. At least, that was the plan. But the first time round it went horribly wrong. What do you think happened?

a) The hurricane got even stronger.

b) The hurricane suddenly changed course.

c) The hurricane fizzled out and died.

ANSWER

b) The hurricane suddenly changed course and hit a town that wasn't supposed to be in its path. A second attempt in the 1960s worked better. Project Stormfury was supposed to weaken hurricanes in the Caribbean and USA. And it seemed to work. It slowed the winds in Hurricane Debbie by almost a third. Meanwhile, in northern Mexico there was a terrible drought when it should have been raining. The authorities blamed it on the project. They claimed that it was messing about too much with normal rainfall patterns. Whether or not they were right, seedy Stormfury was shelved.

Storm-proof building

So if you can't stop the storm, protection must be best. You can make yourself more comfortable by building a storm-proof house. In parts of the USA, there are rules about how strong buildings should be to weather a storm. But how do builders choose the best materials to use? By testing them out in tornado-force winds, of course. Here's how a group of wind engineers in Texas tried to tackle the problem from the safety of their laboratory.

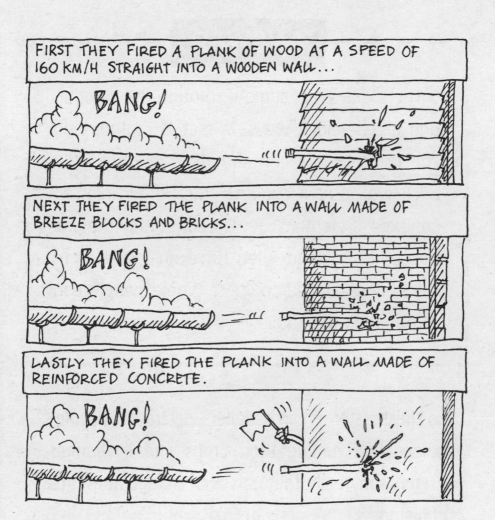

Which material worked the best?

3 The plank went straight through the wooden and breeze-block walls. In fact, a real tornado can fire a steel plank straight through a solid brick wall. But it couldn't crack the reinforced concrete. Scientists now recommend that all houses in Tornado Alley have an inside room made of reinforced concrete where people can sit out a tornado attack.

So sinister storms can be killers, destroying people's homes and ruining their crops and livelihoods. Pretty grim, really. They can even change the course of history.

Earth-shattering fact

In 1588, a five-day storm scuppered the Spanish Armada. A fleet of 130 warships had been sent by King Philip II of Spain to attack and invade England. Only sixty ships limped back to Spain, their mission a total failure. The rest had been dashed against the rocks by ghastly gale-force winds.

STORMY SUPERSTARS

Apart from bringing a few nasty surprises like death, destruction, chaos and catastrophe, has stormy weather ever done anyone a favour? Er, well, yes, stormy weather can be good for you. To prove it, here's a huge list of three whole reasons why:

Good storm guide

It's official that…

Stormy weather keeps you warm. The sun's rays don't heat the Earth evenly. It's baking hot at the equator because they hit directly. It's cold at the poles because they strike at a slant. Good old stormy weather helps share out this heat and stops tropical places getting too horribly hot and the poles too teeth-chatteringly cold. How does it do it? The answer is blowing in the wind. Winds carry spare heat from the equator towards the poles, and perishin' polar air towards the tropics. Talk about blowing hot and cold.

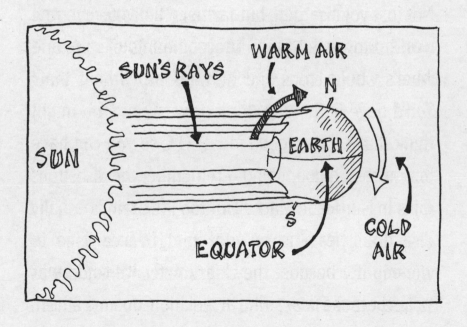

SUN

SUN'S RAYS

WARM AIR

N

EARTH

S

EQUATOR

COLD AIR

Stormy weather makes your garden grow.

LIGHTNING CAN BE BLOOMIN' GOOD NEWS FOR GARDENERS. IT MIXES NITROGEN AND OXYGEN GASES IN THE AIR AND DISSOLVES THEM IN THE RAIN. THE RAIN FALLS AND SOAKS INTO THE SOIL WHERE IT MAKES A FANTASTIC FERTILISER FOR THIRSTY PLANTS.
AREN'T STORMS BRILLIANT?

Not just your garden, but farmers' fields all over the world. Storms let loose huge amounts of rain, and where would crops and humans be without that? You'd have nothing to drink or wash in. (You might think that's a very good idea!) OK, so you can have too much of a good thing – remember the disastrous rains in Hurricane Mitch? But too little rain is equally disastrous. Rain is so vital that people used to worship it as a god. The angry Aztec rain-god was tempestuous Tlaloc, who lived high up in heaven. He kept the rain in four huge jars which he smashed when the Earth needed a shower. Temper, temper!

Stormy weather created life on Earth. Honestly! Scientists in the USA sent a bolt of artificial lightning through a mixture of gases similar to those in the atmosphere. Hey presto! This produced chemicals called amino acids thought to be the building blocks of all life on Earth. And talking of a long time ago, you sometimes find fossilized streaks of lightning which look like greeny-grey glass. (The posh name for these are fulgurites.) They happen when lightning melts the soil.

Other planets have their share of stormy weather, too. Take Jupiter, for example. The Great Red Spot on Jupiter is a mega-storm, and no mistake. It's an incredible 16,500 kilometres long — though it grows and shrinks over the decades. It's been raging for around 300 years (not even your teacher could match that!) Storms on violent Venus rain down stinging sulphuric acid strong enough to dissolve rocks. Your useless umbrella wouldn't stand a chance! Is it surprising that nobody lives there?

Getting warmer?

It's just as well that storms have some plus points because the future looks set to get stormier. This is thanks — yes, you've got it — to the things we horrible humans are doing to mess up the atmosphere. So just what are we doing to the weather? For a start, we're causing the ghastly greenhouse effect.

What on Earth is the greenhouse effect?

Less than half of the heat from the sun ever makes it to Earth. Instead, it just gets soaked up on its way through the atmosphere. But the Earth stays snug and warm because ghastly gases in the atmosphere stop the heat flying off into outer space. Otherwise our whole planet would be covered in ice – great for skating but would you want that all year round? It works a bit like the panes of glass in your grandad's greenhouse – it lets heat in but stops it escaping. That's why it's called the greenhouse effect.

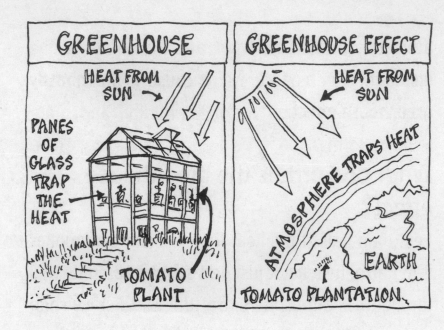

So what's the problem?

The problem is that the amount of ghastly greenhouse gases in the atmosphere is growing. So much that it's making the Earth too warm. Scientists can't agree exactly how much warmer the world will be. They guess the whole Earth will heat up by about 2°C by the year 2050. Which doesn't sound much but it could be disastrous. Even if the Earth gets a few degrees warmer, it could mean stormier weather. There might be more rainfall and more thunderstorms. And if the oceans get warmer, there might be more places where hurricanes could form.

Who's to blame?

The bad news is that we are – horrible humans. Here's how. The main greenhouse gas is carbon dioxide – it's the same stuff you breathe out. It also comes in exhaust fumes from lorries and cars, pollution from factories and power stations, and from burning too many rainforest trees. And we're dumping tonnes of it into the atmosphere. Then there are CFCs (chlorofluorocarbons) from fridges and aerosols (like spray-on deodorants) and pongy methane from rubbish dumps (and from cows' burps and, let's be honest here, farts!). And it's leaving a really bad smell.

What can we do?

The only way forward is to clean up our act! We need to stop burning fuels like coal, oil and wood which all give off filthy fumes. And use cleaner petrol in our cars. It doesn't mean you can stop using deodorant, unfortunately. These days most deodorants are weather-friendly and don't contain any CFCs. Governments around the world have signed up to a plan to spring-clean the planet. And from the year 2000, companies will get certificates to show how much carbon dioxide they have stopped from going into the atmosphere. It's a start but there's a very long way to go.

It's all YOUR fault

Some people feel they have to find someone to blame for their bad weather. When El Niño – a warm current of water – started causing chaos, poor old Al Niño was plagued with complaints. OK so these two letters have been made up, but facts in them are horribly true.

Arkansas, USA,
1998

Dear Mr Niño,

Now listen here, Mr Niño,
What on Earth do you think you're up to?
Ever since we first heard your name, there's
been trouble, nothing but trouble. And yup,
that's definitely Trouble with a capital T.

For months now, we've had rain, rain
and more rain, and storm after storm like
we've never seen before. Now, I'm a reasonable
man, you just ask my friends, but I've just
about reached the end of my tether. This stormy
weather's already ruined my whole year's corn
crop, not to mention those of my neighbours
and friends. Which is serious stuff. Our crops
are our livelihood. And I blame YOU.

Where on Earth is it all going to end?
Now just you stop doing whatever it is you're
doing and leave us all in peace. Or else.

Yours Mr Angry of
..● Arkansas

238

California, USA
1998

Dear Mr Angry,

Thank you very much for your letter. I'm terribly sorry you've been having such a rough time. I so hope it soon blows over for you. But I'm afraid I have to point out that your problems really don't have anything to do with me. It really isn't my fault that it's raining.

Now, I'm wondering, could it be that you've got me mixed up with someone, or something, else? Yes, there are a few people around who've got me confused with EL Niño. My name's Al Niño, you see, short for Alfonso. EL Niño, as far as I know, is a current of unusually warm water which appears off the coast of South America. EL Niño is actually Spanish for child. In this case it means a baby, like Jesus, because it happens at Christmas.

I'm actually a retired naval pilot from California. And if it makes you feel any better, which it probably won't, this year EL Niño's been playing havoc

239

with weather all over the world, not
just in Arkansas.

What happens is this. El Niño makes
the winds blow the wrong way round. And
it also makes more water vapour than
usual evaporate from the oceans, and this
causes more storm clouds to form. So, dry
places have been getting heavy rain, and
places expecting rain have stayed dry.

I don't suppose this is of any comfort
to you, but you might like to know that it's
also caused record rain and floods in
Europe and Peru, as well as a spate of
tornadoes here at home - my own prize
tomatoes have taken a terrible beating.
To be fair, though, it has also cut the
number of hurricanes by half.

I'm sure there's better weather on
the way.

Sincerely Alfonso Niño

A STORMY FUTURE?

So is the weather set to get stormier? Or is all this global warming gloom just a storm in a teacup? Surprisingly enough, it's so hard to tell that even horrible geographers can't agree. Just listen in to these three experts and you'll see for yourself!

Some horrible geographers say:

THINGS CAN ONLY GET WORSE. THE FUTURE WILL DEFINITELY BE STORMIER, AND IT'S ALL DOWN TO GLOBAL WARMING. IT'S MAKING OUR TEMPERATURES RISE BY 2·3°C AND CAUSING MORE STORMS THAT ARE MORE DESTRUCTIVE THAN WE'VE EVER KNOWN! THERE'S NO TURNING BACK, WE'VE GOT TO FACE UP TO THE HORRIBLE FUTURE. DOOM, GLOOM, WE'RE ALL GOING TO DIE!

YEAH, YEAH, SO GLOBAL WARMING'S GOT A LOT TO ANSWER FOR. BUT WE CAN'T KNOW FOR SURE IT'S GOING TO AFFECT OUR WEATHER IN THE FUTURE – IT'S HARD ENOUGH WORKING OUT WHAT THE WEATHER'S GOING TO DO THE DAY AFTER TOMORROW. IT MIGHT GET STORMIER, IT MIGHT NOT. THE WEATHER'S SO UNPREDICTABLE IT'S PROBABLY NOT AS BAD AS YOU THINK. RELAX, CALM DOWN. EVERYTHING'S GOING TO BE FINE!

OF COURSE, IF EITHER OF YOU HAD FOLLOWED YOUR WEATHER RECORDS CAREFULLY ENOUGH, YOU'D KNOW THAT STORMS GO IN CYCLES. HURRICANES DRAW THEIR POWER FROM WARM OCEAN WATER SO COOLER WATER MEANS LESS SERIOUS STORMS. EXPERTS THINK WE'RE REACHING THE END OF A PARTICULARLY STORMY CYCLE, THAT THREW UP MONSTERS, SUCH AS HURRICANE KATRINA, AND STARTING A QUIETER PERIOD. IN THE ATLANTIC, AT LEAST. IT'S A DIFFERENT STORY IN THE PACIFIC WHICH IS SET TO BE STORMY FOR YEARS TO COME.

Hmm! Just who are you supposed to believe? One thing we do know is that stormy weather is horribly unpredictable. You can measure it, record it, prod and probe it until your head's spinning and you're blue in the face. And then, just when you think you've got its number, it goes and does something you really weren't expecting at all. And that's what makes it so horribly interesting.

HORRIBLE INDEX

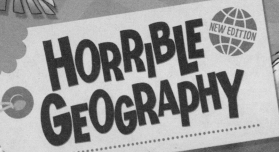

HORRIBLE GEOGRAPHY

NEW EDITION

BLOOMIN' Rainforests

ANITA GANERI

Illustrated by MIKE PHILLIPS

HORRIBLE GEOGRAPHY

NEW EDITION

RAGING Rivers

ANITA GANERI

Illustrated by MIKE PHILLIPS

NEW EDITION
HORRIBLE GEOGRAPHY
VIOLENT Volcanoes
ANITA GANERI
Illustrated by MIKE PHILLIPS

NEW EDITION

HORRIBLE GEOGRAPHY

EARTH-SHATTERING
Earthquakes

STOP

ANITA GANERI
Illustrated by MIKE PHILLIPS

HORRIBLE GEOGRAPHY

NEW EDITION

ODIOUS Oceans

ANITA GANERI

Illustrated by MIKE PHILLIPS

NEW EDITION
HORRIBLE GEOGRAPHY
WICKED WORLD TOUR
ANITA GANERI
Illustrated by MIKE PHILLIPS